ANCIENT PURPLE

Relevant Selections of Latin and Greek
Poetry and Prose in New Translation
with Commentary

by

Tobias M. Goodman

ASPHODEL PRESS
KINGSTON, RHODE ISLAND
AND LANCASTER, ENGLAND

Published by Asphodel Press

First Edition

LIBRARY OF CONGRESS
CATALOGING IN PUBLICATION DATA

Tobias Goodman, 1940-
Ancient purple

212 p. 21.59 cm.
Includes bibliographical references and appendices
1. [to come] 1. Title

2010

ISBN: 1-55921-999-9 CIP [to come]

Front cover illustration Roman copy of an earlier Greek bust of Sappho. Colorized by Chip Phelan (cherrystonetoo@cox.net) to represent the possible painted appearance in antiquity. Back cover illustration: The current faded state of Sappho's portrait. In a fragmentary passage she complains that with age her hair has turned from black to gray.

Printed in the United States of America
Distributed in North America by Midpoint Trade Books,
27 West 20th street #1102, NY, NY 10011
(212) 727-0190, www.midpointtrade.com and
in the United Kingdom, Eire, and Europe by
Gazelle Book Services Ltd.,
White Cross Mills, High Town,
Lancaster LA1 1RN England,
1-44-1524-68765, www.gazellebooks.co.uk

QVIS DEVS HANC MVSAE QVIS NOBIS EXTVDIT ARTEM

For
Ed Pratt
Mason Hammond
Leonard Osler

CONTENTS

INTRODUCTION

I've been lucky in two ways. I was able to be a doctor in a small New England town and developed close relationships which was a privilege which I still cherish, but I have had a second privilege.

For whatever reason, I was in the right places at the right time, and I had the inclination during school and college to study ancient history and literature before going on to medical school. I know that the subject has supported me in both my professional and personal life, and I hope others can find some of the same counsel here.

This volume is not a textbook, but an attempt to share the second privilege that I have enjoyed over the years. It may seem strange to those who have struggled with Latin or Greek verbs that, with all the amusements available to us today, anyone working many hours a day and tired in the evening would seek out a subject that was, well, difficult. Such a pursuit might be appropriate for professional classicists, but certainly not for those living daily life in the real world. Latin might be valuable primarily for training in vocabulary or for mental discipline. Such opinions may be correct, but to have Vergil or Homer or Catullus ready and waiting on the bookshelf like old friends, with all their grace and art and wisdom, and, yes, understanding of today's human condition, has been my secret garden.

The pages of ancient literature have been a source of satisfaction for me, and there I could nourish my hopes, compare experiences, and refine my understanding and expectations. I could go home after work and place a long distance phone call to ancient Rome or Athens.

To be sure there are many possible sources for self- improvement, but I don't think that any thoughtful person, no matter how busy or distracted, ever really abandons curiosity, or does not experience pleasure from a new insight.

I definitely do not intend the present effort to be a serious, scholarly work. Rather I will try to share my pleasures as painlessly and as cheerfully as possible. I have picked what I hope are entertaining or intriguing, mostly short, selections, and have appended my admittedly subjective comments. I encourage you, the reader, to form your own personal conclusions and criticisms. Please do so most of the time. I will add at the back of the book citations for each selection, just in case anyone might want to subject themselves to more of a particular title. I have tried to present some authors who are not so commonly known, or, conversely, less well known lines from the more popular just to interest the reader with something unexpected. Despite my intentions, sometimes I have included more familiar passages because I like them so much.

An exact and literal translation carries over grammar and wording that may seem awkward or ambiguous to the reader. I have tried to convey the meaning of what an author is trying to say in fairly current language. If professional classicists have any criticism of my interpretations or facts, I freely admit any error. Sometimes ancient statements or sentiments are based on cultural assumptions that have changed. These days we would not look down on someone because he was an ex-slave, but would admire his fortitude and good fortune since he was able to escape. Under some circumstances, however, a Roman might think that the background of such a person could make his social value somewhat suspect. Fortunately, such clashes of culture are uncommon in our readings.

Many of us have an image of the Parthenon as in its original form standing a lustrous pure white above the acropolis of Athens. The same thought had been applied to the elaborate frieze of sculpture which was brought to the British Museum through the efforts of Lord Elgin and which have traditionally been called the Elgin Marbles. The museum's care of these famous sculptures has been heavily criticized because remaining traces of the original colors on the surfaces of the figures were deliberately removed. It was thought that ancient sculpture was an idealized monochrome. The development of sculpture in the Italy of the Renaissance, including noble works by famous masters, followed this misconception.

We now know that sculpture, temples, home interiors were actually decorated in bright colors. Hair, lips, eyes, garments were all depicted in realistic shades. The fine skin of a goddess might well be represented by smoothed ivory or polished marble, but that did not mean that her eyes, lips or nipples were of the same color. One can perhaps look at the fine painted sculptures under the eaves of some Hindu temples in India to get some idea of the wonderful, colored effect seen in ancient Greece or Italy. One should think of an ancient temple as something lively and bright, with color and gilding shining in the sun. If contemplating a statue, think for example of a portrait with blond hair and piercing blue eyes, with parted red lips and the flush of youth on the cheeks, looking just a bit past you at something specific.

Comparably the writings of our ancient friends are personal, emotional, immediate, lively, human. The effect varies depending on the author, but in no case do I view an ancient work as a rigid, given testament. The literature should be accessible, not distant, fresh, not formal. I suspect that the relative inaccessibility of the Latin and Greek languages is, in our conception, a little like the fading and bleaching of the temples and the statues of the gods. My humble hope is to reanimate this literature, and here and there add a little of the lost colors, or at least to share a little of the tints that I saw in the evening after the day's labors.

Chapter I

SOME THINGS MEDICAL

Despite the fact that we cannot with certainty identify the famous great plague that took place in Athens during the Peloponnesian War and that is described in Thucidydes' history, there are many diseases familiar to us in ancient medical writings. The general issues of health are still with us since there are still patients with infectious illnesses to be diagnosed and treated, and we still brush our teeth. There were many famous physicians in antiquity, and remarkable surgery was performed as well, but I am not going to present an academic review of ancient medical theories of disease causation or describe the ancient operations for cataract or bladder stone. Here I will present, and comment on, some short selections that I have found professionally interesting.

HIPPOCRATES

THE FIRST APHORISM

Aphorism. A Greek word that means a brief or terse statement of a universal truth. A large library of Greek medical writing has come down to us under the name of the Hippocratic Corpus which contains many works, a few of which may actually be by the hand of, or reflect the words of, the father of medicine himself. Of these, the most popular then and now has been the work entitled *Aphorismoi* or "Aphorisms". Unlike other works, which barely survived, there are 140 manuscripts in Greek alone. As a physician and surgeon, I have found many of the pithy statements accurate and I can sometimes recognize the disease states that they reflect. For example, a statement that the illness will be long-lasting if there are bubbles in the urine seems to refer to cases in which there is a vesico-enteric fistula and intestinal gas enters the urinary tract and is excreted. I can assure you that such a case, without the benefit of surgical repair, will go on for a very long time if the patient does not succumb to sepsis.

I pause now to express my respect. Hippocrates is our great professional parent, the Father of Medicine. His name is attached to the oath with which I swore by Apollo to keep my life and my art pure and holy. (The term "art" or *techne* in this context means a combination of professional skill and knowledge, and is not used to imply creativity.) Sadly, the actual historical Hippocrates is a rather shadowy figure, known more by reputation and works than by careful history, since only later and somewhat unreliable biographies remain. The books within the Hippocratic Corpus contain a variety of medical texts of various dates, authorship, and medical belief. At any rate, it is likely that Hippocrates was born on the Greek island of Cos in 460 B.C., or perhaps a little earlier. He is thought to have lived to extreme old age, but the date of his death is unknown. He appears to have enjoyed a very high contemporary reputation and his assistance was requested even by the king of Persia. He appears to have been an educator of medical students, and is credited with separating medicine from philosophy. His emphasis was on a completely rational approach. He tells us, for example, that epilepsy is not a burden visited on individuals by the gods, but is really an affliction of the brain, something to be treated and not prayed over. As I have said, the biographical materials are not the best, but there are some attractive tales. He was reputed to have been retained by the citizens of the town of Abdera in order to evaluate and treat the purported mental illness of Democritus, who was one of the very first to support the belief that matter is composed of atoms. Hippocrates found the man performing dissections in order to evaluate the possible etiologic role of bile in disease. After evaluating the mental status of the great philosopher-scientist, Hippocrates informed the citizens of Abdera that they were out of their minds not to appreciate the wisest man alive. It may be because of this episode that Cicero, much later, tells us that the term "Abderite" was a synonym for very stupid. Hippocrates is also credited with helping to arrest the great plague at Athens, a claim that seems doubtful in light of other historical information.

Well, all physicians and many others are familiar with the beginning of the first aphorism. The initial words are striking and extremely concise. It has taken me some years to try to understand them in terms of medical practice. Learned commentators have described deliberate obscurities in parts of the Hippocratic Corpus, and have attributed these, in part, to the traditional respect in ancient Greek culture for oracles. Famous examples are the opaque sayings of the inspired priestess at the famous oracle in Delphi, sacred to Apollo. Yet the Greeks knew that for those who listened carefully an oracle could be a clear message.

> Life is short, the Art is long. Timing is precise, experience deceptive, decision difficult. It is necessary to manage not only the medical needs, but also those who suffer, those standing by to help, and external matters.

It is even a little more brief in Greek. To be honest, the first seven words at first seemed to me to be mysterious, but I can tell you what they mean to me now after forty years of practice. I believe that they refer to the inevitable and innate tension between the suffering and fragility of the patient and the abstract thinking that is necessary to formulate a competent plan to help. The statement does not imply that the physician should not be kind, but that he must be the servant of the art as well. It means that there is much to know as a physician and that you had better keep up professionally. The use of the word "long" is not strange; in antiquity, the same word could mean either high or deep.

The subsequent statements in the aphorism deal with these issues: when to intervene, how one can be deceived by the clinical course and the need to balance conflicting factors. These are all familiar issues to those who practice medicine. In a word, the emphasis is on judgment. Does the patient need to undergo a procedure or an operation?

When? Why? What? Are you sure? In surgery manual dexterity, although important and dramatic-appearing, is not as vital as judgment. The ability to make a mature, well-informed and well-founded decision is what makes a good surgeon. At least that is my conclusion after forty years in a surgical sub-specialty. Here Hippocrates hit the mark.

The last sentence in like manner emphasizes issues familiar to the practicing physician. Deal appropriately with someone who is enduring something very unpleasant. Work with those who are helping. Do the nurses understand what you are trying to do? How about the lab? Then there are the external factors. How often in recent years did I have to deal with the hypocrisy of insurance companies and the Byzantine regulations of Medicare in order to obtain what the patient needed! Hippocrates knew that there would always be outside factors with which the physician must deal on behalf of the patient. Despite my frustrations in this area, I did gain some perspective from this aphorism that there have always been non-immediate issues, which a physician has to face.

In antiquity, physicians did not have the microscope and could not see the structure of normal tissue, the pathology of tumors, or the presence of bacteria. Nevertheless, in the Hippocratic Corpus and for centuries thereafter, there was extensive theorizing about human physiology and the etiology of disease. The theories were incorrect, but for a sense of perspective, we may remember that the Hippocratic bedside description of a patient with pneumonia remains accurate today. Pneumonia remained a common, serious and often-fatal disease for millennia, and together with other infectious intestinal diseases may have killed more Union soldiers than Confederate rifle fire. For all those years, our civilization knew of pneumonia. Then German lens makers developed the compound microscope in the nineteenth century, and shortly thereafter, a specific etiology for the lung inflammation in the form of bacteria, a tiny vegetative life form, was discovered. It was not long afterward that, in turn, specific treatment in the form of antibiotics was invented. The mortality rate fell. What a technological spin-off!

Current technologies such as computers have an effect now on medical research, but what they may bring in the future I cannot tell. One hopes that they will assist even more than at present in our future understanding and management of malignancy.

PLINY THE ELDER

CASE REPORTS

The senior Pliny was a very capable administrator and was well liked by the emperor Vespasian. He had a very busy and successful career beginning with command of a cavalry squadron on active duty in Germany. He practiced law, was an honest tax collector in the provinces, and finally was admiral of the naval forces based at the northern end of the bay of Naples. Despite this very active life (A.D. 23-79), he was an incredibly prolific writer; his nephew, Pliny the Younger, described for us the Elder's books and work habits. He wrote about the javelin as a cavalry weapon, a biography of Pomponius Secundus (a benefactor), twenty books about the wars in Germany, a discussion of oratory, about questionable language usages, and other history. All of these works are lost, but we can feel a little better because his great *Natural History* has survived complete in all thirty-seven books.

This large production contains an amazing compendium of facts and anecdotes covering much if not most of what was then contemporary knowledge about the earth: astronomy, geography, human biology and society, terrestrial and aquatic animals, trees, crops, flowers, medicines, painting and art history, stone, and gems. Some of the information we would today place in the category of traders' or even old wives' tales. Other data hint at what may be useful, but forgotten, knowledge. Still other statements are unbelievable or simply impossible. Sometimes amidst the huge mass of material, indifferently collected, lies a surprising nugget. Thus after a list of monstrous human oddities including far-off tribes with feet pointing backwards, barking people with the heads of dogs, one-legged jumpers, tribes whose members routinely live past two hundred years of age, men with furry tails, and a less extreme discussion of triplets and other subjects, Pliny remarks:

> It is not just a fable that women are changed into males. We find in the formal chronicles that during the consulship of Publius Licinius Crassus and Gaius Cassius Longinus (167 B.C.) a maiden still with her parents was turned into a boy and then banished to an uninhabited island at the direction of the seers. Licinius Mucianus related that he himself saw at the city of Argos one Arescon, formerly called Arecusa, who had even been married, then developed a beard and masculine features, and then was remarried to a wife. Licinius himself also saw a boy of the same type at the city of Zmyrna. And in the province of Africa, I myself saw Lucius Constitius, a citizen of the town of Thysdritum, who had changed into a male on his wedding day.

At first sight, this statement seems to represent more uncritical reporting by credulous observers. It is a not uncommon experience for a urologist to be called to the neo-natal unit to examine a newborn infant whose external genitalia are, as we say, ambiguous. In our era, we have learned that there are three kinds of gender determinants: genetic, somatic and social. Normally chromosomal or genetic sex is determined when sperm and egg meet. The female is given an XX complement and the male XY. After about seven to eight weeks of growth in the uterus, the development of the male internal and external genital apparatus depends on the endocrine function of the fetal testis. If this effect is absent or weakened, the female predominates. Actually, looking at the externals of a seven-week fetus, one could not tell boy from girl.

Like everything else in life, sometimes things go wrong. A male pseudohermaphrodite is an individual who has normal (both X and Y chromosomes) genetic sex, but presents a feminine appearance because for some reason the action of the fetal testis has been blocked. Yes, there are a variety of complicated reasons for this occurrence. In the human body, the male hormone testosterone is produced in a series of chemical steps from cholesterol. If a certain enzyme is absent,

A rather seductive-appearing Hermaphroditus asleep on a pillow. This divine being was often graphically depicted in ancient art with both male and female characteristics. There is a series of ribald wall paintings in Pompeii which show the disappointment of a lusty God Pan as he removes Hermaphroditus' bedclothes.

then a step is blocked. In two of the deficiencies (of seventeen beta-hydroxysteroid oxidoreductase and five alpha-reductase if you must know), individuals at birth have either normal-appearing or almost normal- appearing female genitalia, and are assigned to a female social role. Some of the more ambiguous situations might be diagnosed in an institution with the needed training and lab facilities, but in a more traditional society and certainly in antiquity, the newborn would be viewed as little girls. However, since these individuals still possess testes (usually not apparent), at puberty masculinization, sometimes fairly complete, occurs. Muscle mass increases, male distribution of body hair develops, including beard growth, the voice lowers and the attitude changes as well. In some patients, fertility has even been documented. This kind of biologically based gender reversal has at times attracted intense attention and dramatization from the media. One example might occur when an athlete has competed as a female and won high standing and a medal in a national or international competition. The individual has been raised as a female and thinks of herself as a woman, but her appearance seems atypical to observers. Considerable confusion and controversy results when testing demonstrates the presence of a Y chromosome.

Seen in this light, Pliny's descriptions now become more believable and may actually be the first case reports of these conditions. Of course, our friend living in the first century A.D. could not have known about the sophisticated science behind our current understanding of these difficult medical and social issues. In view of the population densities in the Mediterranean world in antiquity and the etiology of some of these defects only requiring that the patient be homozygous to develop the problem, I am personally convinced that these are true case reports. In the last case described above by Pliny, the masculinization had, I am sure, begun at puberty and was only revealed in the social situation of a marriage.

I wonder how many other small truths are to be found in the mountain of material in the Natural History. I have always suspected that some useful drugs lurk in Pliny's pharmacopoeia, but going through everything line by line is challenging. Sometimes it is difficult just to identify what animal or plant it is about which he is commenting. He does give us very impressive lists of his sources, all available before the great losses of the middle ages, and now sometimes just names. I suspect that somewhere in his thirty-seven books there is more to be learned.

SCRIBONIUS LARGUS
TOOTHPASTE AND TESTIMONIALS

Callistus, an emancipated slave, had an important administrative role under the emperor Claudius and may even have been involved in planning the assassination of the previous emperor, the mad Caligula, in A.D. 41. It was to this official, who had the ear of Caesar, that Scribonius Largus dedicated his book of prescription formulas. At that time, there were no large drug companies and physicians specified the composition of the medications they advised. Custom compounding was a fairly common practice when I was in medical school, and I was instructed in how to write a prescription to specify what I wanted formulated. The practice became much less popular, but appears to be returning to a degree. Pharmacists are certainly very capable in this area (I had three uncles who were pharmacists and I admired their skill and humanitarian dedication), but there may be some government regulation, and complex custom formulation would have to be profitable for the controlling large business chains.

Scribonius' dates are probably about A.D. 1 to 50. Through the influence of Callistus, he appears to have accompanied Claudius on his famous invasion of Britain in A.D. 43. Otherwise, we know little about our man. I would guess that his education was primarily medical, since his Latin style is, shall we say, technical. Nevertheless, to my medical eye, he does seem to have some experience in the treatment of various conditions, many of which I can recognize. Some of his formulations seem to me to be potentially effective and to make sense. He uses squill, which has a digitalis-like active ingredient, for congestive heart failure, and offers anticholinergics and antacids for ulcer disease.

By this time in the early empire, society was changing, and, as the historian Tacitus puts it, sycophancy was swelling. The power and the purse of the *princeps*, or first citizen as the emperor was artfully styled, led to the increasing centralization of patronage. The interest in, and the influence of, the imperial family increased as time went on. Thus, we have an apparently well-trained physician-pharmacist fawning on the ex-slave functionary of the emperor.

Today the concept of celebrity endorsement is all too familiar. Shoes, perfume, soap, shampoo and even toothpaste are all recommended by someone famous, rich or powerful. A former candidate for the office of President has praised the efficacy of an erection- enhancing pill. I don't have to give you more examples. Now the Romans, in their personal lives, had the same needs as we do, and, yes, used toothpaste or powder. Our author's list of formulations did include some instructions on how to make dentifrice, but, as you will see, not just anything ordinary. The Latin word "*dentifricium*"is a compound of the two words from which our English "dental" and "friction" derive. To the Romans, dentifrice was a paste or powder with which to scour and polish the teeth. Contemporary pastes and powders still contain among other things a binder and an abrasive. Scribonius preserves the following recipes for us.

> . . . for a dentifrice that makes the teeth white and strong: you need to sprinkle vinegar mixed with honey onto a pint of barley flour and to knead it a long time and when done divide it into six small balls. Separate these and mix in half an ounce of rock salt. Then cook in an oven until reduced to ash. Then you will need to grind up the balls and mix in as much spikenard as needed to produce an agreeable scent. Octavia, the sister of emperor Augustus, used this. . .

> . . . Very many as well make use of this dentifrice: they pick the glass pitcher-rubbing herb when it is in seed with as much root as possible. On the first day, they wash and dry it. On the next day, they steep it in fresh concentrated brine. On the third day, they wring it out and pack it into a new jar. Then they set into it a sort of tiers of rock salt. When it is thus prepared, they cook it thoroughly in the furnace used to heat the hot water for baths until it is reduced to ash. Then, after it is ground down to two thirds of its volume, they mix in an appropriate amount of spikenard. This whitens the teeth and also strengthens them. For sure Augustus used it. And our god Caesar's Messalina uses this: one pint of stag horn burnt to ash in a new jar, an ounce of Chian gum mastic, and an ounce and a half of Egyptian rock salt from the oracle of Ammon.

Gum mastic, an aromatic plant resin is still produced on the island of

Messalina and child. A formal portrait with dynastic implications, but the sculpture group was completed before her political eclipse and death.

Chios. Some fairly recent research indicated that gum mastic in the mouth significantly decreased the formation of dental plaque. Spikenard, as you may guess, adds a covering aroma.

Now for a little gossip about these female members of the Julio-Claudian royal family. Octavia, the sister of Octavian, who later became the emperor Augustus, appears to have been a paragon of virtue, and was much respected in her own time as well as in later ages. After her first husband died, she married Mark Antony, in an attempt to support the power-sharing arrangement between him and her brother. In reality, the two were competing for control, and the dissipated Antony quickly left Octavia for Cleopatra, who controlled the resources of Egypt. In Rome, Octavia continued to live in Antony's house, support his family interests, and later even nicely brought up the children of the defeated and dead Antony and Cleopatra. Her great-granddaughter Messalina, however, was tragically and scandalously different. When she was very young, perhaps still in her teens, she was married to Claudius who was then about age fifty and subject to unattractive neurological deficits. She had two children by him, and then it seems could not handle the corrupting influences that swirled around the center of power. We are told that she had innumerable lovers and forced the handsomest man in Rome to divorce his wife. She overplayed her hand when, with Claudius still ignorant of the goings-on, she celebrated a form of marriage to this individual who was consul-designate. This final development, implying the possibility of a coup, was viewed as a threat to the safety and illicit profits of her emperor-husband's ex-slave administrators. They made sure that Claudius was finally fully informed of the lurid details of her behavior, as well as the personal threat to himself. The historian Tacitus describes Messalina's activities with her paramour at a wild and decadent party while Claudius was being told all. She was soon killed on the orders of one of the emperor's assistants, as the softhearted Claudius was vacillating about what should be done. She, elaborate toothpaste or not, in turn then became a byword for excess in her own time and later. The satirist Juvenal had her sneaking out from the palace to a brothel where she could not satisfy her physical desire no matter how hard she worked, and Pliny the Elder, in the tenth book of his Natural History, recounted a story about her winning an all day and all night sexual competition with a top prostitute after twenty-five copulations.

Chapter II

HISTORY

There are amazing heroes and villains, triumphs and tragedies to be found in ancient history. Some of the events and characters are endlessly fascinating. I have read well conceived studies about history - what it is and how we should think about it, but, for me, reading these documents, which indeed probably lie somewhere between a story and a factual record, allows me to share an experience, and for me that is enough. I have picked some passages here, which show personality, as well as drama, in the events depicted, but readily admit that they are some of my personal favorites.

SIMONIDES

THE THREE HUNDRED

What were the most famous lines in antiquity? There is probably no real answer to that question, but I will make a guess.

Simonides, our subject poet here, was a voluminous writer, but now only exists in quotations found in other authors, in short pieces in a famous anthology, and in fragments on shreds of papyrus. A recent discovery of just a few more lines on papyrus has generated much interest and learned comment.

Simonides was born on the Greek island of Ceos, probably in 556 B.C. He lived to be almost ninety years old, and wrote in a variety of genres. He wrote verses about the battles of the Persian wars, eulogies, songs, epigrams, and epitaphs. The poet Theocritus, no mean author himself, termed Simonides a god-like bard. Others, however, complained that he wrote for pay and was a tightwad. His work was highly valued for its style and the manner in which it aroused emotion. Cicero comments that he was learned and wise. Plutarch recalls the statement of Simonides that he often felt regret after speaking, but never after remaining silent. He was known also for his memory and he developed recall techniques.

Cicero also recounts an intriguing story all the details of which we may or may not believe. It seems that around 515 B.C. Simonides was a guest in the palace of a ruling family of a town called Crannon in a northern territory of Greece. He had been hired to compose some verses, which he then declaimed at a formal dinner before the head of the family, a man named Scopas. We are told that he followed the usual custom of poets and enriched his verses with a great deal of material about the heavenly twins, Castor and Pollux. (You may recall that by the favor of Zeus they shared immortality. At times, they would put in a personal appearance in order to intervene as saviors at critical moments. Their most famous exploit in this regard was their assistance to the Roman army at the storied battle of Lake Regillus around 500 B.C. This latter episode was retold during the nineteenth century in fine style by McCauley in his *Lays of Ancient Rome.*) After Simonides had finished his presentation, Scopas said in a very vulgar manner that he was only going to pay half of the previously agreed amount, and that the remainder should be requested from Castor and Pollux since they had been equally the subject of the poet. The story goes on that a little later Simonides received a message that a certain two young men were at the outer door of the building, and demanding to see him. He got up, went out, but did not see anyone. Meanwhile the roof of the hall in which Scopas and his relatives had remained fell in, and they were killed. Some believe that the heavenly twins paid their debt by saving the poet's life; others tell the tale, but do not accept the epiphany.

Simonides had a long and varied career and lived in different cities. He died in Syracuse and was buried in Sicily, but may have been in Athens during at least part of the Persian Wars. It may have been there that he wrote his famous epitaph for the tomb of Leonidas and the three hundred Spartans who fell at Thermopylae.

The last stand of Leonidas and his three hundred, as told by Herodotus, outshines any retelling or film dramatization. I picture the Persian king, with his army of three hundred thousand, overconfident and laughing at the Spartans who were carefully combing their hair before the battle, and the king not quite believing that they wished to look presentable before killing or being killed. I remember the defensive battles in the narrows before the traitor Ephialtes betrayed the secret path with which it was possible to march behind the Greek position, and then the final act, the determined fight to the end by the surrounded and vastly outnumbered Greeks. I first read of this action at the age of ten or eleven and was quite moved. For me it still raises issues of freedom against tyranny, what free men can do, the importance of one's word and of courage. I knew then, as I know now, that I could not emulate such behavior, but the story does turn the mind to contemplation. One can only guess what Simonides, who saw the extinction of a tyranny in Athens and the establishment of democracy, might have thought, and how he came to write the lines that so many in ancient times knew.

Oh stranger! Send a message to the Spartans
That we lie here, obedient to their words of command.

NEPOS

A NAVAL STRATAGEM

Cornelius Nepos was born in northern Italy around 110 B.C. and lived until about 24 B.C. He is thus another writer of the late Roman republic but does not have as much reputation for style or talent as Lucretius, Catullus or Cicero. He seems to have written with an eye towards a less educated readership, perhaps those who had not learned Greek or knew little Roman or foreign history. I have viewed him as also perhaps showing a little of everyday Roman stolid literalism. Much of his work is lost, but the accident of history has given us his book on outstanding foreign commanders. Most of the individuals whose careers are summarized therein are Greek, but Nepos does include sketches of two Carthaginians, one of whom is Hannibal.

Hannibal Barca (the surname is thought to mean "lightning") was the brilliant general of Carthage, the city on the North African coast that was Rome's long-term enemy. Nepos recounts the dramatic story of Hannibal at the age of seven being required by his father to swear eternal enmity to the Romans on the altar of the god Baal. In 218 B.C., with an army that included thirty-seven war elephants, he made his famous crossing of the Alps and invaded Italy. He defeated three Roman armies in succession and nearly destroyed the Roman nation. He remained a threat and stayed in Italy until 202 B.C. but was eventually beaten by Roman courage, patience, and persistence. He fled to the Eastern Mediterranean where he advised other enemies of Rome, who were then in turn defeated as well. He ultimately moved on to the court of King Prusias of the principality of Bithynia in North-west Asia Minor. This king was at war with a Roman ally named Eumenes, king of Pergamum, a city more to the East in Asia Minor. Hannibal is portrayed by Nepos planning his usual alliances against the Romans, but it seems that Prusias was outclassed.

> Eumenes, king of Pergamum, was very close to the Romans and was hostile to Prusias; war both on land and sea was being waged between the two. However, in both environments Eumenes was prevailing because of his association with the Romans. Therefore Hannibal wanted all the more to overcome Eumenes, since he thought that once he had eliminated him, everything else would be easier. He undertook the following scheme to defeat Eumenes. In a few days there was to be a naval battle. Hannibal had fewer ships. He had to do battle with a stratagem, since his armament was inferior. He commanded that as many live poisonous snakes as possible be gathered together and collected into clay containers. When he had finished a large number of con-

tainers, on the day on which the naval battle was to happen, he called together his naval personnel and instructed them to attack only the ship of Eumenes, and to consider it entirely adequate just to hold off the others. They would be able to accomplish this latter mission easily because of the large number of snakes. He himself would arrange things so that they would know which ship carried the king. He promised that he would reward them handsomely if they either captured the king or killed him. After he had exhorted his men, the fleets on both sides were launched for combat. When each side had arranged a line of battle, before giving the signal to engage, Hannibal sent out under a flag of truce a messenger in a small boat who would demonstrate Eumenes' position to his own side. When the messenger reached the ships of the opposition, he held up a letter and declared that he was looking for Eumenes. He was immediately led to the king since no one had any doubts that he had come for anything besides peace. After the commander's ship had been made quite evident to his own side, the messenger went back where he had come from. However, when the letter was opened, Eumenes found nothing in it except ridicule. Although he wondered about it, and could not figure out the explanation, nevertheless he did not hesitate to commence hostilities at once. When the ships rushed together, all of the Bithynians, according to Hannibal's command, attacked Eumenes' ship. Since the king could not withstand the force of their attack, he ran for safety, which was only to be had by withdrawing inside the defensive positions that had been erected on the adjacent shore. Meanwhile, when the rest of the Pergamene ships were pressing in on their opponents very strongly, suddenly the clay containers, which I mentioned above, began to be hurled into

> them. When these were first thrown they aroused laughter in the fighting men, and they were unable to figure out what was happening. However, after they observed that their ships were filled up with snakes, they were very frightened by this new predicament, and since they did not see how they could get away from the snakes, they reversed course and returned to their naval base. Thus, Hannibal prevailed over the armament of the Pergamenes by a stratagem . . .

Hannibal's strategy of eliminating the hostile commander was effective at gaining a victory in the ancient world. From time to time Hollywood rediscovers the idea of snakes in an enclosed space, but I think with not as much success as that which Hannibal achieved. The Romans, who recognized his talent, feared him, and I suspect that many years after his death, small Roman children were threatened with Hannibal if they were not good. If we imagine that Hitler had invaded the United States and had a military presence here for almost two decades before his eventual defeat. . . well you get the idea. Hannibal was a man of great ability; it is too bad that he was on the side of Carthage, of a people who really did burn babies as a sacrifice to their god in their religious rites. The name Hannibal probably means something like "blessed or favored by Baal".

CICERO

THE VILE DEGENERACY OF MARK ANTONY

Marcus Tullius Cicero. The middle name was his family name and from it, he was called "Tully" in eighteenth century England. One reason may have been the name by which he is familiarly known now or *cognomen*. Originally these were nicknames, familiar appellations, that came to indicate a family branch of a clan. Such nicknames could refer to a variety of personal achievements or characteristics such as a military victory, baldness, being handsome or lucky. For example, the family nickname "Cato" derives from the Latin adjective *catus* and

A modern painting recreates the sccene at the time when Cicero delivered his first oration against the solitary and sinister Catiline. Cicero saved the Roman state from a destructive conspiracy, but set the stage for his own exile and then murder later on.

means clever or shrewd. Cicero it turns out refers to *cicer* which is a chick-pea or garbanzo.

Our Cicero was born in 106 B.C. in the country town of Arpinum. He was given a state of the art education in Rome and Athens by his successful father, and served through the series of elected Roman offices to the highest position of consul despite not coming from a known political family with a tradition of public service. Such descent was a normal background for a political career at the time. It was as consul that he detected and crushed the conspiracy of Catiline (63 B.C.), and left us four famous speeches in which he convinced the Roman senate to save the state from an evil man and his followers.

Actually a total of fifty-eight speeches survive, from different periods in his life and about different subjects and people. In addition, there are copious other works: many on rhetoric and philosophy, and hundreds of personal letters, most of which were actual communications and not planned for circulation or publication. They are a treasure trove of social and historical as well as personal information, and allow us to reconstruct some of the stirring events of two thousand years ago almost day by day. They do give us a glimpse of Cicero as a person, including his failings, and he has been criticized for these, but I see no reason why because he was involved in great events he should be expected to be perfect as well. It is with equanimity that I can see him overly excited about collecting a work of art, betraying uncertainty and compromising on matters of principal. I am realistic enough not to expect perfection from every physician, pilot, priest or politician in our own time. There is no reason to demand that figures in history be faultless.

Yet no one can deny that Cicero was a great orator. His use of language and construction of sentences were marvelous. He has endowed us with a gift of great literature of trans-generational magnificence. Nevertheless, we should remember that he worked and wrote in a difficult time during the death throes of the Roman republic. In the years before him, there had been increasingly wide and wild swings of the political pendulum between populists and supporters of the status quo. There had been alternations of control based on the increasing power of professional Roman armies, and marked by confiscation of property and wholesale political murders called proscriptions. By the time of Cicero all knew that final decisions could at any time be made by recourse to armed force and that debate would be moot. Please keep this point in mind when you read the selection that I have prepared for you, but first let us review a little historical background leading up to this passage.

Caesar, having been appointed to the old office of dictator, died at the hands of upper class conspirators who feared he wished to be king on the famous Ides, or fifteenth, of March 44 B.C.; he was stabbed by many hands in the senate house. One of his close lieutenants was Marcus Antonius, known to us in Shakespeare as Mark Antony. He had been brought up in the house of a stepfather who had been executed previously by Cicero as a co-conspirator with Catiline. After the death of Caesar, there was considerable jockeying for position and advantage in the resulting power vacuum. In the summer of 44, Cicero had planned to leave for Greece, but returned when informed of important political activity in Rome. He made a moderate speech in the Roman senate against Antony who responded with accusation

A bust of Mark Anthony. He is blamed for the murder of Cicero and was Cleopatra's lover after the death of Ceasar. You can decide for yourself if he looks self-indulgent.

and vituperation, and the gloves were off. During the period of October and November Cicero prepared his famous second "Philippic" which actually was never delivered and was probably more a political pamphlet somewhat like Thomas Paine's writings during the American Revolution. In the first portion, Cicero defends himself against Antony's unfounded accusations; he continues with a remarkable compendium of personal insult. He describes Antony's depravities, corruptions, greed, robberies, cowardice, and lies. In the lines that follow, Cicero discusses what happened when Antony takes over, or steals, the country home of Varro, the famous scholar of Latin literature, two of whose works, one dealing with the Latin language and the other with farming, actually do survive. The contrast between the imagined intellectually profound activity of the owner-academician and the orgiastic debauchery of Antony is dramatic and highly emotive. It is even more affecting when one remembers that he was also a consul at the time, due to the favor of his patron Caesar.

> Who says that Varro's estate at Casinum was even for sale? Who saw the sign for that alleged auction even displayed? Who heard the call of the auctioneer? You say you sent someone to Caesar in Egypt to buy it from him. No doubt, it was a burden to wait for him. In truth, did anybody ever hear that anything from Varro's property was stolen? For it was his safety that concerned the majority of people. Why? If Caesar also wrote to you and told you to give it back, what can be said about such indiscretion? For a little while take away those swords that we see; now you comprehend that an auction of Caesar is one thing, that your overconfidence and recklessness another. Indeed not only the owner, but any friend, neighbor, guest or superintendent will keep you at a distance from that estate.
>
> Yet during how many days in that villa did you revel in the most degenerate manner? From early in the day there were drinking, amusements, vomiting. Oh wretched house with an unsuited owner! Although how can such as he be an owner? Rather it is possessed by one unsuitable! Certainly, Marcus Varro wished it to be a sanctuary for his studies, not for lusts. Previously what had been said in that villa? What thoughts had been there? What had been written down? The laws of the Roman people! The written memorials of our ancestors! An account of all wisdom and of all teaching! But in fact with you as the lodger - not really the owner - everything resounded with the cries of drunkards, the flooring tiles streamed with wine, the walls were soaked, free-born boys were busy with hirelings, whores with family

> matrons. People came from the local towns of Casinum, Aquinum, Interumna to call formally; no one was let in. Indeed that was just; the emblems of consular distinction were degraded in the vilest of men.

There is much more to this piece and Cicero nowhere lets up on his target, Mark Antony. There are fourteen of these *Philippics* in total. Most of them do not contain this degree of invective, but they all were designed to rally strong political opposition to the then consul Antony. Cicero tried to use the current political leaders who wielded real power in the form of troops to form a "concord of the classes," but was outmaneuvered when a group of three combined in a power-sharing compromise. A proscription, a series of political murders in which the names of those designated for destruction were placed on written lists, followed. Magnanimity had died with Julius Caesar, and any favorable attitude towards Cicero was overwhelmed by the enmity of one of the three. Just below, in the single surviving fragment of one individual's work, we shall see a description of the result. The murderous purges of the nineteen thirties in Nazi Germany and the Soviet Union did not represent innovation in political life, although in this case the fame of the victim was exceptional.

CORNELIUS SEVERUS

THE DEATH OF CICERO

It is a very sad fact that we only possess a tiny portion of what was written by the Greeks and the Romans. Everything was copied by hand on twenty-foot long rolls of a kind of paper made from stems of the papyrus plant. These were stored rolled up and gradually unrolled as one read along. Books were copies of copies of copies. All books were limited in number and fragile. Authors' works existed in small numbers at the best of times and by the time of the Middle Ages were subject to endless mutilation, erasure and extinction.

We will see that the dynamic Catullus, by a lucky chance, squeezed through in one manuscript. His friend and literary equal, perhaps even superior, Calvus, is gone except for bits and pieces. However, there was another way that an author's work, or samples of his work, might continue to exist. A writer in order to make a point might quote another author who was popular, or just might add appeal and artistry. It is for this reason that we possess the lines of Sappho that we will read in Chapter V. Even Pliny the Elder, in his weighty *Natural History*, quotes some lines of verse. The archetype of an author who repeats the words of others is the elder Seneca. He had, as he tells us, an extraordinary memory, and could repeat a list of two thousand names spoken to him all at once. Drawing on this memory, in his old age he wrote a large number of selections from various speakers and writers with whom he had been familiar years before. He preserves for us some descriptions, which otherwise would have been lost, of the tragic political murder of Cicero. Among these are twenty-five striking lines by Cornelius Severus who lived at the time of Augustus and was a friend of Ovid. We really know nothing about this Cornelius, but to judge by this little that we have, the destruction of his work represents an immeasurable loss.

I must include here a small explanation of the names towards the end of this piece: King Perseus was a dangerous enemy of Rome, and commanded the same type of Macedonian phalanx with which Alexander had conquered the Persian Empire. Syphax was a Numidian tribal chief, who actually fought the great Scipio Africanus (victor over Hannibal), as well as Masinissa, with some success. Jugurtha was another very successful foreign chief who took advantage of some Roman weaknesses. Hannibal himself was the great man of dread for generations of Romans. With many obvious differences, he could be thought of as nested in the Roman mind as is Hitler in ours. Catiline and his associate Cethegus were from fancy patrician families, but plotted bloody revolution because they needed money. Earlier in his career, Cicero had saved the Roman state from them. Mark Antony needs no introduction. It is said that after Cicero was murdered his head and hands were stuck up on the speaking platform in the center of Rome for all to see.

The heads of brave men, almost breathing, rest on their
very own speaking platform,

Reading a Greek book roll around 440 B.C. Such books could be twenty to thirty feet long. The connected papyrus sheets were unrolled from the right hand and rolled up again in the left.

But, as though the only one there, the vision of liquidated Cicero eclipses the others.
Then we remember the mighty deeds of a consul's heart, and the band of conspirators,
And the detection of the criminal compact and the eradication of the patricians' iniquity.
We remember the punishment of Cethegus, and Catiline deprived of his evil promises.
Of what use were popularity or years filled with public office?
A lifetime perfected in sacrosanct skills?
A single day carried off the ornament of the age
And the expressiveness of the Latin tongue was struck by sorrow and silent in sadness.
Once the only protection and safety for those in trouble,

Always the eminent head of the nation,
He was the defender of the senate.
The public voice of justice, of laws, of custom, of civil affairs,
Was muted for eternity by savage weapons.
A fellow-citizen, who arrogantly trampled down the distorted face
And the white hair spotted with the blood of desecration
And the holy hands, agents of great works,
Gloated, but forgot about the treacheries of fate and the gods.
In no age to come will Mark Antony atone for this act.
A milder victory did not inflict the like on Perseus of Macedon
Or on you, scary Syphax, or you Phillip our enemy.
There was no derision at all during the triumph over Jugurtha
And even when cruel Hannibal fell before our wrath
He still carried his body parts intact to the shades of the underworld!

PLINY THE YOUNGER

DEATH OF PLINY THE ELDER

As you might guess, Pliny the Younger was a close relative, actually the nephew, of Pliny the Elder. Born in A.D. 61, he lost his father at a young age and was adopted by his famous uncle. He was very successful, practiced law, and occupied several senior administrative posts. One of his goals, however, was a form of book immortality, and he cultivated friendships with various authors such as the poet Silius Italicus and the great historian Tacitus. Pliny published in succession nine books of his letters, which, together with another book added after his death, have survived to our time. Unlike the copious letters of Cicero, they are not primarily personal communication, but polished exercises designed to be a form of literature. The letters contain details about contemporary life, political events, trials, murders, descriptions of daily life, friendly or contemptible individuals, literary concepts, even ghost stories.

I have included the letter below because it is so popular and concerns a subject of continued interest, but please observe that there are deliberate rhetorical constructions and flourishes, and that it is carefully balanced to make a whole. I think that when he talks about a pine tree, Pliny means one of the shape that is so commonly seen in Italy and not a North American white pine. Some think that when Pliny says "landslide from the mountain" (the Latin word is *ruina* meaning a falling down) that it refers to a pyroclastic flow. I will leave that to the vulcanologists. The events described here by Pliny occurred in A.D. 79.

Pliny to Tacitus, greetings.

You ask me to write to you about my uncle's passing so that you can hand down a truer report to those who come after us. I thank you because I see that eternal honor for his death is to come if you write about it. For although he perished, as did masses of people and cities, due to a great disaster in a beautiful area, and is always going to be sort of memorable because of that remarkable event, and, although he himself had written very many works that will endure, the immortality of your compositions will still add much to his everlasting remembrance. I truly think that those whom the gods have given the gift of either doing what must be written down or writing down what must be read are blessed, but are really most blessed if they do both. My uncle will be in this last group, both in his own and in your books. It is for this reason that I am all the more happy to take on what you have requested. No, I even beg to do it.

He was at the northern promontory of the bay of

Naples, being there in command of the local fleet. On August 24 in the early afternoon, my mother informed him that a cloud of unusual size and shape had appeared. He had enjoyed the sunshine and a cold bath, then reclined to eat, and was studying. He ordered his sandals and climbed up to a location from which he would best be able to view this wonder. Those observing the cloud from a far distance could not tell from which mountain it was rising, but later it was seen to be Vesuvius. The cloud was assuming a shape that resembled nothing so much as a pine tree. After being carried up to the heights like a very long tree-trunk, it was then spreading out with some branches. I think this was because it was lifted up by a fresh breeze, then no longer under the influence of the weakening breeze, or overcome by its own weight was dissolving out sideways. Now it would be white, then dirty and patchy as if it had supported soil or ash.

To that most learned man it seemed to be something great that should be examined more closely. He ordered a light Liburnian galley to be prepared, and he gave me the opportunity to come along if I wished. I answered that I preferred to study and by chance he himself had assigned what I was writing. As he was leaving the house, he received message tablets from Rectina, wife of Bassus, who was beside himself over the threatening danger, since his villa lay nearby and there was no escape except by boat. She was pleading to be rescued from such jeopardy. My uncle changed his plan, and continued with high resolve that which he had begun scholarly intent. He launched large galleys with four banks of oars. He went on board himself to bring help not only to Rectina, but also to many others, for there were numerous fine estates along the shore. He hurried to that area from where everyone else was escaping, and held a straight course towards the danger, so unconcerned that he could comment on and record all the occurrences and all the shapes of that evil event just as he was able to observe it.

Then ash fell onto the ships, the nearer he approached, the hotter and thicker it was. Then also pumice stones, black and broken and scorched with fire, then unexpected shallows and a shoreline obstructed by a landslide from the mountain. He hesitated a little as to whether he should turn back, then he said to the pilot who was advising such a course of retreat: "Fortune favors the brave! On to Pomponianus!" He was at Stabiae (a local resort) separated by the middle of the bay where the sea flows in gradually along the shore that curves and sweeps in. There, although not yet close, the danger was apparent, and would increase and be imminent. Pomponianus had stored his luggage in his boats hoping to escape when the opposing wind subsided. My uncle was carried to that location by the wind that was, however, favorable for him. He embraced the anxious Pomponianus, comforted him, encouraged him; my uncle ordered himself to be carried down to the bath in order to alleviate his host's fear by his own peace of mind. Having bathed, he reclined; he dined either quite cheerfully or, what is equally fine, appearing to be cheerful.

Meanwhile, in many places on Mount Vesuvius, broad flames and lofty conflagrations were shining out, whose brilliance and brightness were enhanced by the darkness of the night. In order to calm everyone's fear, my uncle pronounced that the fires were left by the frightened rustics and that abandoned villas were burning in a state of desertion. Then he went to bed, and in truth he slept soundly. For his breath sounds, which because of his heavy-set body were rather heavy and noisy, were heard by those guarding his door. But the court-yard which led to his suite was now filling up with ash and a variety of pumice stones so that it would not be possible to get out if he stayed any longer in his bedroom. He was awakened, went out and rejoined Pomponianus and the others who were staying up. They took council together as to whether they should hold their position indoors or wander around in the open. Indeed the building was shaking with frequent and enormous quakes, and, as though it were being pulled off its supports, seemed to sway and rock back and forth. On the other hand, outside falling pumice stones, although lightweight and eaten-through, were a cause of concern. Still when they compared the threats, they chose the latter option. My uncle was motivated by objectivity, the others by what made them less apprehensive. They covered their heads with cushions, which they tied on with linen. This was for protection against the material that was falling on them.

Elsewhere it was already day; where they were was a night blacker and more opaque than all other nights. However, many torches and other light sources helped. They thought it was right to go out onto the beach and see close up whether by then the sea was accessible. Until that point in time, it had remained rough and unfavorable. My uncle lay down there on linen fabric that had been thrown on the ground, and once and then again ordered and drank something cold. Then fire and the odor of sulfur, the precursor of fire, put the others to flight and awakened him. He stood up, leaning on two slave-boys, and immediately fell down. My surmise is that his breath was blocked by very dense fumes and his windpipe, which in his usual condition was weak, constricted and often intermittently inflamed, was obstructed. When day returned, the third since he had last seen daylight, his body was found untouched, unharmed, and covered with the clothes he was wearing. The appearance of the body was more like one sleeping than dead.

Meanwhile, my mother and I had remained at the northern promontory of the bay of Naples. However, this is not material for history, nor did you desire to be informed about anything more than his passing. Therefore, I make an end here. I will add only one thing, that I have related only that for which I was present or what I heard immediately after the fact, when it was fresh in memory. You will select what is the best. It is one thing to write a letter, another history, the one to a friend, the other to everyone. Farewell.

When I first read this letter, I was fascinated by the eyewitness account, and then I began to wonder what did happen to Pliny and his mother when they were left behind. I read on and after going through three more letters which dealt with such things as manners at a literary recital, a legal case and land prices, I came to another letter to Tacitus, who, it appears, had the same curiosity. The Roman name for the northern promontory of the bay of Naples was Misenum. Campania is the name for the surrounding county. In some of his other letters, Pliny sometimes admits that he himself is not all bad. You will, I am sure, notice that in this letter which follows he does seem to show himself in a favorable light.

Pliny to Tacitus, greetings.

You have informed me that when I wrote you the letter that you had requested about the death of my uncle, you were induced to want to know more about not only the apprehension but also the hazards that I experienced when I remained behind at Misenum since I broke off when I touched on that. As Vergil writes in the Aeneid: "Although my heart is revolted by the memory, I will start."

After my uncle had left, I spent the rest of my time on my studies since that was the reason why I had stayed there. After that I took a bath, I ate, and then had a restless and short sleep. Earthquakes had occurred previously over many days, and were not worrisome since they were common in Campania. In fact, they got so much stronger that night that one would have thought that everything was not only severely rocked, but wrecked as well. My mother burst into my bedroom just as I was getting out of bed, and thinking that she was still asleep. We settled down in the courtyard of the house, which separated the sea from the buildings by not a not very large distance. I am uncertain whether to call it perseverance or recklessness; I was in my eighteenth year, but ordered up a book of Livy's history, and read it as though it were just leisure time for me, and even made selections as I had been doing previously. Then, lo and behold, my uncle's friend, who had recently arrived from Spain, saw me and my mother sitting there, especially me reading, and started to criticize her forbearance and my lack of concern. I continued to apply myself to the book no less intently.

It was by now early morning and the daylight until then had been uncertain and sort of weak. Already the surrounding structures were wobbling; since we were in a place that was open but still narrow, we had an immediate and definite fear of a collapse. Then we finally decided to leave town. The common people followed along horrified, and preferred someone else's plan of action, which during a panic is like prudence. They formed a large troop, pressing hard upon and pushing those who were leaving. After we left the building, we came to a halt; there we experienced many wonders and many terrors. For the carriages, which we had ordered to be brought out, were being forced in opposite directions, and would not stay still in the same place even when stabilized with stones. Besides that, we were watching the sea being sucked back into itself and sort of driven back by earthquakes. In fact the shore had advanced and had doomed many marine creatures on dry sand. Off to the side, a black and fearful cloud was rent by twisted and fluctuating fluxes of fiery exhalations, and was splitting open as though into long sheets of flame, which were like lightning, but much bigger.

Then that same friend from Spain really said more tartly and more insistently, "If your brother, if your uncle is alive, he wants you to be safe. If he is lost, he wanted you to survive. Therefore why stop going?" We answered that we were not going to act so as to take council about our own safety when we were not sure about my uncle's. He did not hesitate any longer, but rushed off and made a mad dash to take himself away from danger.

Not long after, that same cloud lowered itself over the dry land and concealed the sea. It had enveloped and hidden Capri, and it took out Misenum after overflowing it. Then my mother started begging, encouraging, ordering me to get away by whatever means possible. A young man could do it, but she was weighed down by her age and her corpulence, and would die happily if she knew that she herself were not the reason for my death. I was saying that, on the contrary, I would not be safe unless we were together. Then I clasped her hand and made her quicken her pace. She complied unwillingly, and blamed herself because she was slowing me down. And there was still at that time fine ash. I looked back. Opaque pitch-black was closing in behind our backs, following us and spreading over the land like a flood. "Let us turn aside," I said, "while we can still see so that we are not thrown down in the road by the mob following us, and are not trampled in the dark. We had barely sat down and it was night, not as it was moonless or cloudy, but as in a closed-up space when the light has been extinguished. You could hear women screaming, babies crying, men shouting. Some were trying to find their parents, some their children, some their wives by the sound of their voices. Here they complained of their own misfortune, there that of their family. There were some who were impelled by the terror of death to pray for death. Many prayed to the gods. More concluded that the gods were nowhere and that this was an eternal and final night for the cosmos.

And there were also those who magnified the real dangers with fabricated and deliberately false alarms. There were some who reported that something had collapsed at Misenum, that something had burned, falsely, but they were believed. Little by little the light came back. It did not seem like daylight to us, but an indication that the fire was coming closer; in truth, the fire remained far away. Again, there was darkness, again much heavy ash. At intervals, we got up to shake it off. Otherwise, we would have been covered up by the ash, and even squeezed forcibly by its weight. I might be able to pride myself that amid such dangers I did not moan or utter a cowardly word, except that I must have been thinking that I, with everything and that everything with me, was going to perish: a sad but still great consolation for being resigned to die.

Finally, the darkness sort of thinned out into vapor and mist and passed off. Presently it was true day, and the sun was even shining, but pale such as during an eclipse. Everything that met our still fearful eyes was changed, enveloped in deep ashes like snow. We made our way back to Misenum and took care of our physical needs in whatever way we could. We finished a night uncertain and doubtful between hope and fear. Fear predominated, since the earthquakes continued and for many frantic individuals their own and others' misfortunes were made ridiculous by frightful prophesies. However, we still then did not plan to leave, although we had suffered the danger and were expecting more, until there was report of my uncle.

You will read this letter, which is in no way suitable material for history, and not use it for your writing; you must blame yourself who certainly made the request if it does not even seem suitable for a letter. Farewell.

SUETONIUS
THE DEATH OF JULIUS CAESAR

Many have heard of the phrase "the Twelve Caesars". This term has led to a minor historical confusion. There were many, many more Roman emperors than twelve. In the year A.D. 69 alone there were four. Actually, the term is a title that is often attached to the biographical sketches of the first twelve Roman emperors, which were written by the author Suetonius, who was a friend of Pliny the Younger, and was born around A.D. 70. He had a legal and literary career, and we learn a very few details about him in Pliny's letters. For a time Suetonius held the chief secretarial position under the then current emperor and probably had access to the letters and records of earlier emperors. He wrote many scholarly works on subjects such as nature, time, language, traditions, but only the nearly complete *On the Lives of the Caesars*, a work that was published around A.D. 120, has survived. These biographies are made interesting by their remarkable details, as well as by what, at times, is rather hostile gossip. He was even able to quote from family letters about private matters, and presented particulars about personal appearance and habits.

The first emperor that Suetonius described was Julius Caesar. You may be interested to know that Julius was not his first, but his family name. His full name was Gaius Julius Caesar. "Caesar" was a family branch *cogmomen*. Suetonius details Caesar's extraordinary abilities and talents as well as his love affairs, including the famous Cleopatra. Caesar is described as being tall, of fair complexion, with piercing dark eyes and well-formed limbs. Apparently, he was vain about his increasing baldness and combed his hair forward. He is depicted as a great orator, an able author, a skilled general and brilliant tactician. Suetonius further describes him as being skilled with weapons and horses, of great physical bravery and endurance, and as a merciful, loyal and inspiring leader. However, Suetonius does present another side and tells how, in a nation that was at least nominally still a republic, Caesar accumulated too much power and glory. After he defeated Pompey and the senatorial party in a civil war, he was in complete control and accepted a continuous consulship, became "perpetual dictator", took on names such as commander and father of the country, had his statue placed among those of the kings of early Roman history, had a seat of gold in the senate chamber, and even had a month (our month of July) named after him. These and many other assumptions of power led many of the senatorial class to fear that he was aiming to be king in reality. Suetonius tells us that small groups of two or three formed a conspiracy of over sixty individuals; the leaders were Gaius Cassius, Decimus Brutus and Marcus Brutus. Those who have read Shakespeare's plays on the subject will here be on familiar ground, although it is thought that Plutarch's biographies may have been his main source. I do think, however, that Suetonius' version is adequately dramatic. At the point where we join Suetonius' story, the conspirators have been considering where and when to do away with Caesar, and a favorable opportunity becomes apparent.

After the senate had announced a session for the fif-

Gaius Julius Caesar. the great general and dictator. A man of formidable intellect and ability, but a potent force in the destruction of the Roman republic.

teenth of March in the meeting-hall of Pompey, the conspirators readily selected that time and location. However, definite portents forewarned Caesar of impending doom. A few months earlier, when a settlement was being founded at Capua under the Julian law, and the colonists were taking apart some very old tombs to construct country-houses, they were going about it all the more enthusiastically because with careful inspection they had found a goodly number of vessels of ancient manufacture. On a sepulcher in which Capys, the founder of Capua, was said to be buried, a sheet of bronze was found inscribed with Greek words and letters with this meaning: whenever the bones of Capys should be uncovered, the result would be that a descendant of Troy would be slain by the hand of blood relations, and then would have his revenge in a great calamity for Italy. Lest anyone should think this matter to be a fable or invented, my source is Cornelius Balbus, Caesar's closest confidant. In the days closest to the final event, he found out that the herds of horses, which he had dedicated to the river Rubicon when he crossed it, and had let go free without a keeper, obstinately kept away from their fodder, and wept profusely. In addition, the fortune-teller Spurinna warned him as he was performing a religious sacrifice that he should beware danger, which would not extend beyond the fifteenth of March. On the day before the fifteenth, birds of different species from a nearby grove of trees followed a little kingbird, which had entered the meeting-hall of Pompey with a small branch of laurel, and tore it to pieces. On the actual night before the day of the assassination was to dawn, in his sleep Caesar thought he saw himself flying for a time above the clouds, and then at another time to shake hands with Jupiter. His wife Calpurnia fancied that the roof of their house collapsed and that her husband was stabbed in her embrace. And suddenly their bedroom doors opened by themselves.

Because of these things, and because of a concurrent indisposition, he vacillated a long while about whether he should stay home and delay the matters he had intended to bring before the senate. At length, when Decimus Brutus persuaded him not to ignore the numerous senators who had already been waiting for him for a long time, fairly late in the morning he sallied forth, and he included a note, held out to him by one individual he met that disclosed the conspiracy, with other petitions, which he was holding in his left hand, as if he were about to read them shortly. Subsequently, after many animals had been sacrificed, although he was not able to obtain a favorable omen, he scorned the tradition, and entered the senate house. He mocked Spurinna and accused him of being fallacious, because the fifteenth of March had come without any injury to himself. Spurinna said that even though the date had indeed come, it had not passed by.

In a show of doing their duty, the conspirators stood around Caesar as he was sitting down, and right away Cimber Tillius, who had agreed to act first, approached more closely as though he were going to make some request, and, as Caesar was shaking his head and was motioning for postponement to another time, snatched his toga from both shoulders. Then as Caesar was calling out, "This is really brute force!," one of the Cascas wounded him from behind, a little below the neck. Caesar seized Casca's arm and pierced it with his writing instrument; He tried to spring forward, but was hindered by another wound, and when he observed that he was attacked by drawn daggers on all sides, he covered his head with his toga, at the same time with his left hand pulling down the garment's folds over his lower legs so that he would fall more honorably with even the lower part of his body covered. It was thus that he was stabbed with thirty-seven wounds, having said nothing

> except a single sigh at the first blow, although some write that when he saw Marcus Brutus coming at him he said in Greek, "And you, son?"

Thus, Gaius Julius Caesar, at the height of his power, permanently appointed to the office of dictator, the very word meaning that his word was law, died suddenly and violently. This dramatic fall from the peak of human success to the rites of a funeral is a reversal of fortune familiar to Americans. An assassin's bullet instantly dispatched President Lincoln just at the successful conclusion of his civil war policy. So died John Kennedy more recently. There are all too many others. General George Patton suffered an untimely death after being fatally injured in an automotive accident, while on duty in Germany, about seven months after the end of the European war. At the end of the conflict he had received high honors for his brilliant feats of command. He has been a controversial figure to some, but I can tell you that for many years in my office the patients would tell me, with great pride, in response to my query about their military service in their medical history, "I was with Patton" if they had served with the Third Army. My father, who was also a physician, told me that one of his friends, a neuro-surgeon, had been flown to Germany for consultation, and found Patton's spinal cord injury to be inoperable. Maybe there is something in human affairs that necessitates sudden and violent death at the peak of success or glory.

Nevertheless, I can tell you about an earlier "death" suffered by George Patton, one that I have not seen in any of the history books or biographies. When I was in training forty years ago, I had the privilege of working with Dr. Richard Alt, one of the finest surgeons and medical personalities that I have ever known, at the local hospital in Beverly, Massachusetts. He knew of my interest in things historical, and one day in the conference room requested an old chart from 1939. It was brought to him and he told me to look at it. The name on the chart was George S. Patton, and the occupation was listed as army officer. Dr. Alt confirmed that indeed it was the chart of General Patton who at that time was a colonel. I believe he was then the senior colonel in the United States cavalry. Dr. Alt then told what happened in what I now remember to have been the summer or late summer of 1939. He was called to the emergency suite to see a patient with a new fracture; I think it was a broken tibia, the large leg bone just below the knee. When he arrived, there was Colonel Patton on an examining table in riding clothes. He told Dr. Alt that he had been playing polo at the Myopia Hunt Club and that his horse "threw him." Dr. Alt noticed that there were tears on the colonel's cheeks. He expressed sympathy for the colonel's pain and said that he would get him some morphine right away. The response was some four-letter words, which embellished a statement that the pain was nothing. The colonel feared that, when unspecified enemies in Washington found out about the injury they would force him to retire. He had been waiting in the peacetime army for over twenty years since the Great War; there was a war coming in Europe, he could sense it, and he would miss it for medical reasons. Dr. Alt considered this statement and then basically said, "Do we have to tell them?" They agreed to keep it a secret, and the colonel was admitted to the hospital; the fracture was reduced and a cast was placed on the leg. He did well at first, but in those days they did not practice early ambulation, and kept patients in bed. After a number of days, I don't remember how many, Dr. Alt happened to be in the hospital and was called on an emergency basis to the floor with the report that Colonel Patton was dead. My doctor friend ran there and found the patient blue with no pulse and no blood pressure. He told me that all they had at that time was intracardiac epinephrine; he grabbed a syringe with a long needle and injected the medication into the colonel's left ventricle. Patton took a breath, and his color improved a little. They found a pulse and his blood pressure began to creep up. He survived what Dr. Alt diagnosed as a pulmonary embolism. At that point, I looked at the vital signs sheet in the clinical chart; it was very neat and showed an orderly progression of normal pulse and blood pressure readings, and then no heart rate and a pressure of zero over zero. Then I could see an initial very low blood pressure followed by some steady improvement, not up to normal, but enough to keep Patton alive. The rest of his stay was marked by continued improvement and stabilization, and finally he was discharged home in good condition. They kept the pulmonary embolism a secret, too. Later on that fall he returned to his duties, and one can read in the books that he was transferred to armor and was promoted to brigadier general the following year and major general in 1941. After that, he liberated Sicily, and played a major part in getting the German army out of France. In December of 1945, he did not escape death again.

I do not mean to imply, by telling this story, that Patton was a Caesar, but he did talk about reincarnation and the belief that he had been a warrior in past lives. I hope that he was right, and that he is with us now in some form. I am afraid, however, that the conflict between genius and the prejudices of officialdom is still present.

Chapter III

MYTHOLOGY

"Myth" these days is a term used casually to describe an idea or story that is not true. However, classical myths are the sometimes beautiful Greek and Roman stories about gods, heroes, heroines, and events derived from tradition or the imagination. There have been many theories about these myths: that they are the echoes of the subconscious mind, or the remnants of forgotten historical events, or of early religious ritual. The presence or absence of truth or falsehood in these stories we shall have to discover.

For me personally classical mythology has always been about the human experience presented in idealized form. Just put yourself in the position of Paris, peacefully guarding his flocks on the mountain when suddenly he is confronted with three goddesses, beautiful, all-powerful female entities, and has to pick one as the best, or at least the prettiest. Whatever he does, he loses. Does that kind of situation sound familiar? Ultimately, myth can tell us a little, or a lot, about human behavior, and may also reflect the deepest fears and hopes of a society. For me the gods and goddesses of the Greeks are often recognizably human in their various travails.

Well, that is my argument. I will now try to defend it with what follows.

HYMN TO ARTEMIS

SACRED AND STRONG

In antiquity, there was a balanced belief in both the male and the female divine. When one grows up in a monotheistic society, there may not be the same expectations about idealized gender roles as if Aphrodite and Athena were seen to play an active part in the everyday fluctuations of public and personal events. Among the Romans, there were certain religious rites that only women could perform and attend, and upon these the safety of the state was believed to rest. In their form of polytheism, the Greeks and the Romans thought there were more divine influences behind occurrences than just the will of Jupiter whose name is a form of *Diespater* or "sky-father".

I have always liked the simplicity and the stature of early Greek as well as Roman literary productions. There is an appealing freshness and communication in any such writing before school training polishes and perfects artistic statement. We have a collection called the *Homeric Hymns* which actually may be preludes to other longer recitations and which are not of the same age as the Iliad and the Odyssey; the latest are probably before 400 B.C. They contain a variety of subjects and divinities. The goddess Artemis (the Roman Diana) was, like her brother the god Apollo, the child of Leto and fathered by Zeus. You may remember the story that Zeus was attracted to Leto and she gave birth first to Artemis and then later Apollo while pursued everywhere by jealous Hera. Artemis was the maiden huntress, of great feminine beauty and grace but dangerous or deadly if crossed. An expert archer, she quickly saw to the destruction of the luckless Actaeon who was out after game with his dogs and who had the misfortune of catching sight of her disrobed and bathing. A finely painted vase in the Boston Museum of Art shows her lethal grace. Artemis also seems to have been involved in the death of Adonis, Aphrodite's movie-star-like favorite. Thus she is a female figure of unearthly beauty, forever unwed, a most skilled hunter of beasts and sometimes men, and certainly a figure to be respected and propitiated. These characteristics helped to generate the language of the following hymn.

I sing of Artemis, of the golden bow, hunting cries all
around her,
Revered maiden, deer-striker, arrow-lover,
Pure-blooded sister of Apollo of the golden sword,
Delighting in the chase, down the mountain shadows

Artemis, serene and beautiful, punishes Actaeon who had seen her disrobed and bathing. She turned his own dogs on him and then transfixed him with arrows.

and windblown hilltops
She bends her all-gold bow, and shoots a shaft of woe.
The mountaintops of the lofty peaks quake in fear
And the thickly shaded forest resounds fearfully with the cry of wild creatures.
The earth and the fish-generating sea shudder.
But she, remaining bold-hearted, turns in all directions to kill the stock of wild animals.
Then whenever she is satisfied with searching for them
And she is in good spirits, she unstrings her well-curved bow

And goes to the great mansion of her beloved brother
Phoebus Apollo,
To the fertile territory of Delphi, where she choreographs
The beautiful dance of the Muses and the Graces.
There, after she sets down her curved-back bow and arrows;
Putting on elegant attire, she directs and leads the dances,
Where they send out divine fragrance
And praise in song Leto of the beautiful ankles,
And how she gave birth to children beyond compare
In the deliberations and deeds of the deathless divinities.
Greetings to you, oh daughter of Zeus and fair-haired Leto . . .

TRIPHIODORUS

FABRICATING THE TROJAN HORSE

Many of us are familiar with the Iliad and the Odyssey, which deal respectively with a limited period of time during the Trojan War and the tribulations of Odysseus' homeward journey. These two works appear to have formed parts of a large so-called "Epic Cycle" that included six other long poems, which described the whole of the war and which, except for fragments and short summaries, are lost. Whether Triphiodorus had access to the material of the *Little Iliad* in primary or secondary form is uncertain, but he seems to have been a Greek grammarian and epic poet who lived in Egypt around a thousand years after the time of Homer, perhaps in the fourth century A.D. or later. (I should say here that, after the death of Alexander the Great in 323 B.C. and until the defeat of Antony and Cleopatra in 31 B.C. Egypt was ruled by a Greek-speaking Macedonian dynasty. Under Roman and then Byzantine rule, Greek remained to a great extent the legal and literary language until the Arab conquest.) Triphiodorus (traditionally and less correctly spelled Tryphiodorus) wrote a variety of epic works of which only 691 lines on the capture of Troy remain extant. He began this surviving work by outlining the situation in the tenth year of the Trojan War, which started after Paris ran off with Helen. At this point Achilles and Hector have been killed, and still the walls of Troy stood firm. He then described the divinely inspired construction of the wooden horse.

At this time the craftsman Epeius guided by the goddess Athena
Constructed against Troy an ornamental image of a huge horse.
Planks were cut and brought down to the flat plain
From the very Mount Ida where earlier Phereclus had constructed ships
For man-defending Paris which was the beginning of the evil.
He made a hollow belly fitted between very wide sides,
As big as a ship curved up left and right, rounded off straight down the line for length.
He fastened on a neck to the hollow chest,
Smearing yellow gold over the purple hair of the mane;
The erect hair ran in waves down from the head and was pressed in by the bridle.
And he set in eyes of precious stone in two concentric circles
Of blue-green beryl and blood-red amethyst
Which combined to sparkle in double colors
So the red eyes were circled with blue-green precious stones.
Into the jaw he notched silvery teeth
As though all ready to bite down on the ends of the well-plaited bit.
And in the great mouth he opened up invisible passages
To keep breath flowing back in for men hiding inside

And for life-giving air to waft through the nostrils.
Very erect ears were fastened to the upper temples
Always ready and waiting for the trumpet-call.
He fitted the back and pliant spine appropriately to the flanks
And positioned the hips next to the polished-smooth rump.
The tail trailed low to the bottom of the legs,
Drawn down with tassels just like a grapevine.
The feet seemed to go forward under the dappled knees
As if they were designed to get ready for a fast race.
So while they seemed to press forward, in reality they had to stand unmoving.
Below the legs, the hooves displayed gleaming tortoise-shell curved around them,
As they barely touched the plain with their powerful bronze.
He attached a door that could be closed and a well made ladder,
Not only joined to the side in a way that the noble steed
Could carry an armed force of Greeks in various directions,
But also that when released and firmly set
It would spring out as a passage for them
Down from above and up from below.
He strapped a purple-flowered harness around the horse,
And the twisting curves of a controlling bridle fastened with ivory
And silver-chased bronze down around the white neck and sides of the face.
But after he had completed the work on the foe-resisting horse,
He placed under each one of the feet a well-armored wheel

So that the horse could be controlled when drawn along on the flat plain,
But not find the way difficult when it was pulled with force on a road...
And so, wide and high, it shone with dread and much beauty.
And Ares as a horseman would not have despised riding it if he had come across it alive.

You are probably wondering why I have included this description of the well-known Trojan horse, from a passage which is difficult enough to need some effort on my part to render it intelligible to myself and to you. Well, we know that the Trojans brought the horse into their city with singing and dancing and ignored the deadly menace within it. They look stupid to us, but there are not too many surviving versions that inform us that the horse was made to look beautiful and that its glorious appearance hid its reality. I think that in greater or lesser terms we continue to make similar mistakes. We all do it. I certainly do. I have done it. I think I still do it. We are fooled by a shiny car, a beautiful or handsome face, an appearance enhanced by fine clothes, colorful packaging of products, an attractive politician or political program, even just repainted surfaces. There are probably endless examples of things that are not quite what they seem to be, but are decorated in one way or another to deceive our hopes. Perhaps a detail about the Trojan horse, its flashing eyes, its purple and gold mane, something or other, will stick in our memory, and remind us to be careful.

QUINTUS SMYRNAEUS

CASSANDRA

Priam, who was king of the losing side during the Trojan War, had three daughters, the most beautiful of whom was Cassandra. She was so beautiful that the god Apollo desired her and as a present endowed her with the gift of accurate foreknowledge. She still turned him down. He did not or could not take back her perfect ability in prophesy, but arranged things so that no one ever believed her.

Another late Greek author, Quintus Smyrnaeus, about whom we know almost nothing, but who probably wrote during the third century A.D., wrote a fourteen-book poem that continues from the point where the Iliad leaves off. He recounts events in the last year of the Trojan War such as the combat between Achilles and Penthesilea, the queen of the Amazons who had come to help the Trojans, and later the death of Achilles himself at the hands of Apollo. Smyrnaeus describes the final introduction of the hollow horse filled with hidden warriors into Troy itself. He then presents the impassioned and frenzied reaction of Cassandra who was always right but never believed. And now the horse of death is in the city:

> But no fear troubled the hearts of the Trojans
> Even though they could see clearly disturbing omens spreading through the entire city.
> In fact, their fate erased the sanity of them all
> So that while they feasted they would be struck down by the Greeks,
> And complete the full measure of their doom.
> One heart alone was sure and certain.
> One mind was lucid, Cassandra's.
> The words she spoke were never false,
> On the contrary, they were genuine.
> Destiny made the interpretation of her words like the blowing of the wind
> So that Troy would be destroyed.
> When she perceived the signs of ruin throughout the city,
> All the harbingers of the same approaching doom,
> She uttered a great cry like that of a lioness
> That a man hunting eagerly among the thickets
> Has wounded or hit with a missile.
> Her heart rages in her breast

—a line missing here—

. . . along all the . . . the lofty mountain,
Her strength exceeds its limits.
Thus, with the spirit of prophesy within her throbbing and impatient,
She lets herself out of her chamber.
Her hair spread over her shoulders and upper arms, and fell down to her back.
Her two eyes flashed in defiance,
And lower down her neck undulated to and fro
Like a tree-trunk in the wind.
The well-born maiden indeed groaned and screamed loudly.
"O you wretched people!
Now we have passed into the darkness below,
For around us the city is filled with fire
And blood as well, and our dismal doom.
In every direction the deathless gods show us sorrowful omens,
And portents of destruction while you drink your wine.
Obstinate are you! You know not your dreadful destiny,
But you all senselessly make merry at the same time.

—a line missing here, a possible reference to the horse—

While it concealed a great calamity!
But you will not be persuaded by me,
Not even if I harangue you over and over.
And so the Furies, angered by the disastrous affair of Helen,
And the implacable Fates flit throughout the entire city.
During your banquet, a meal of pain, you are feasting
On your last suppers defiled with foul blood.
You are already skirting the very same path as the shades of the dead."

My goodness, what a dire prediction! And no one paid any attention. Nobody at a happy party would want to stop and listen. We moderns never make a mistake like that. Do we? Is there something vaguely familiar about disregarding an unexpected or apparently improbable warning? Did anyone take notice when for years a man with financial expertise tried to warn the authorities and the public about the Madoff financial fraud? I remember another example, one a patient told me about his father. When Colonel Thorpe sent a telegram in late 1941 from his liaison post in the then Dutch East Indies and warned of a coming attack on Pearl Harbor, was he believed? His son, who was in his eighties at the time of a visit to my office, began to tell me about his father who retired as a major general after the war. His father had been an old Pacific army professional, and in 1941 was a liaison officer in Jakarta. The Dutch theater commander, a field marshal, unexpectedly came into the colonel's office, told his secretary to leave, and then secretly informed him that the Dutch had broken the Japanese radio code and that an attack on Pearl Harbor was planned for early December. The field marshal added that he thought that Colonel Thorpe's superiors in Washington might want to know about it. The American considered the situation and was concerned that in turn the Japanese might have broken his own radio code. He therefore put the information into cable code with his associate, the naval liaison officer, and wired to Washington. They waited, but received no acknowledgment, became concerned and so sent a second cable. When there was still no response, they sent it a third time and then got an answer. "Don't send us any more cables." I actually did hear about this pre-war Dutch intelligence success from two other elderly Dutch patients over the years. I suspect that, without my belaboring the point further, that you can think of other examples, perhaps even in your own personal life. Probably even now someone is predicting a future, avoidable, negative event, but we are not listening. At least the story of Cassandra does give us some perspective when we so often and so pompously in our courts and congressional hearings criticize and pursue those whom we deem negligent, but of course always, always, retrospectively.

However, when times are good, and one is partying, and there is laughter, and the ice clinks merrily in the glass, no one wants to hear of doom and destruction. Such a message, and the one bearing it, are never welcome. If you see the future too clearly, you are not desirable company. What is this thing, attractive and garlanded with flowers? It cannot be the horse of Troy. No, it is desirable, just like a professionally packaged, ah repackaged, securitized mortgage. Of course this observation is in retrospect as well.

Now if only Apollo would whisper in my ear and tell me what might be today's deception. Then I might be able to share a particular and concrete warning, but for certain no one would listen

Chapter IV

SOCIAL COMMENTARY

Perhaps in the preceding pages, I have convinced you that myths have something to tell us about the feminine, about misrepresentation, and about risk. Beyond mythology, there was outright Greek and Roman social commentary, sometimes extending into satire or political opinion. Like today, such writing often took the form of literary statement rather than scientific sociology, although attempts were made in that direction. My selections here are more memorable than scientific, but may be of some interest. They are from a wide time frame which should tell us that people always like to talk about these things.

LUCIAN

EARTH VIEWED FROM THE MOON

By now, all of us have seen the famous view of the earth photographed as United States' first long distance manned spacecraft was in orbit around the moon. The earth appears very blue and beautiful against the darkness of space and the desolate features of the moon. In antiquity, educated individuals were well aware that the earth was a sphere, and I think of that photograph when I read the satire of Lucian in which he describes a visit to the moon by one Menippus and depicts events on earth as seen from a distance. Lucian was a prolific writer of the second century A.D.; much of his work has survived in addition to sometimes interesting forgeries attributed to him. His work is critical of hypocrisy and often very amusing. For example, he creates conversations between the Olympian gods, which deal with their embarrassing foibles. He renders philosophers ridiculous, with long beards and wrinkled brows having serious discussions in complicated language and coming to opposite conclusions. His adventure tales that are designed to mock impossible contemporary fantasies may be the first science fiction stories with trips between planets included.

The earth to the moon story that I have selected begins with the character of Menippus, who himself was an earlier writer who described human folly and whose books have been lost. He reports the story of his trip off the earth to a friend. He states that he was irritated and confused by all the different versions of the universe propounded by the different philosophers, and decided to go and see for himself. He made himself wings and soared up to the moon from which he could look down at the earth, which he tells us looked very small from that distance. We enter at the point at which he has got himself oriented as to what he is seeing. I have here excerpted two passages.

Menippus:

> . . . when once I intently directed my vision toward earth, the entire life of men was apparent, not only by national groups and cities, but even the men themselves, sailing, making war, farming, arguing in court, the ladies, the wild animals, just as many as our sea-girt land supports . . .

A passage follows in which Lucian in the guise of Menippus explains to his incredulous friend that he was given the eyesight of an eagle so that he could, almost as though with what we would call a telescope, spy out small subjects. He then gives examples of royal poisonings, conspiracies, and incest. He says that he could see in royal palaces:

The N.A.S.A. Picture of the earth seen from the moon. Lucian would have liked this image.

> . . .those committing adultery, murdering, scheming, stealing, swearing falsely, frightened, betrayed by their nearest kin. While the doings of kings furnished me with such great entertainment, what private parties did was funnier by far. For there in addition I saw the Epicurean philosopher Hermodoros swearing falsely for the sake of a thousand silver dollars, the Stoic philosopher Agathocles suing his student over tuition, the public speaker Kleinas purloining a bowl from the temple of Asclepios, the Cynic philosopher Herophilos lying asleep in a brothel. Why should I speak of the others: those breaking into houses, the bribed, the loan sharks, the freeloaders? On the whole, it was a varied and diversified scene.

His friend now asks Menippus to tell more.

It is impossible to recount all these things in order, my friend, when it was an effort just to see them. Nevertheless, the main points of the matter were such as Homer said were shown on the shield of Achilles. For over here were banquets and wedding-feasts, over there were law-courts and legislative citizen assemblies. Elsewhere someone performed a big sacrifice. Another was eulogizing at a nearby funeral, and when I studied the Getes, I would see them warring, and when I passed over to the Scythians, they were seen wandering about on their wagons. With a slight bend of my vision to the other side, I watched the Egyptians plowing, and the Phoenicians shipping about merchandise, the Cilicians pirating, the Spartans beating on themselves, the Athenians litigating. With all these things happening at just about the same time, you can perceive already what sort of disorder it appeared to be. Just as if someone had arranged many performers and many bands, then, destroyed the harmony by assigning his own music to each of the performers, with each one pursuing his own objective, achieving his own purpose, and eager to outdo the one next to him in elegance. By Zeus, what do you make of this kind of activity?

Friend:

Totally absurd and chaotic!

Menippus:

Indeed, my friend, all of the performers on the earth are like that, and from discord such as this is arranged the life of men who not only howl dissonance, but who behave oppositely, and agree on nothing, up until the time that the director drives each one of them off of the stage, saying he is no longer needed. After that, they are all the same, remaining silent . . .

If you are not familiar with many of the nationalities that Lucian mercilessly depicts you may find it intuitive to replace some of the names with current ones, say the North Koreans and the tenants of Wall Street and then imagine them at their usual activities: piling up excess profits or the bodies of political opponents. You may wish to add into the mix serial killers and politicians, advertising agencies and suicide bombers, art critics and mercenaries, madams and moralists, rich television evangelists and strip-miners, - I am sure you can think of others. We may then compare the conclusions of Lucian with those of our own age. Where we see beauty and unity on a jewel-like earth suspended in space, he saw folly, lies, confusion and deceit. Where we see hope, he saw a squirming anthill. (As a matter of fact, in another page or so from where we have left off, Lucian indeed compares the cities of men to anthills.) I will leave it to you to decide which vision is more accurate.

PLUTARCH

TOO MANY FRIENDS

In our conversation you will become familiar with the statement that one or another author has suffered near extinction and only survives in one manuscript or in small amounts or even just in fragments. This is indeed the condition of many famous names, but there are a few, who, despite some losses, still provide us with a large number of preserved and complete books. Cicero is one of these; another is Aristotle. Despite the preservation of thirty-seven books of his *Natural History*, all of the remaining works of Pliny the Elder are lost. Of Livy's one hundred and forty-two books of Roman history, we have only thirty-four. It is true that some of Plutarch's work is also gone, but a very large amount remains. Many of us have heard of *Plutarch's Lives*, a very fine series of paired Greek and Roman biographies, but we also possess an even larger group of works loosely named the *Moralia*. These writings deal in an educated and urbane manner with a variety of subjects, including such varied selections as advice to newly-weds, the man in the moon, the sayings of Spartan women, the education of children, virtue versus vice, Delphic oracles, controlling anger, why we should not borrow, and so on. Plutarch opposed the teachings of both the Stoics and the Epicureans. In general, he wrote about what he considered proper values and way of life, and human failings and, in our terms, psychology. Plutarch lived from about A.D. 50 to 120 and does seem to have some practical advice, not to say wisdom, on offer, even if his language is influenced by the academic philosophy of his day. Nevertheless sometimes the way in which the advice is couched is quite remarkable and memorable.

Here is a little background on the subject of Plutarch's selection below. In ancient times, friendship was a serious, even formal, business, with social and political expectations and obligations. Cicero, a practical as well as philosophical politician, wrote a detailed essay on the subject in which he tells us that friendship can only develop between those of moral worth and is the helpmate of merit. For him friendship is a mutual understanding of goodwill and esteem, not calculated for personal gain, and should be based on a natural inclination and not advantage. Cicero states that the more an individual possesses independence and high qualities the better he will become a cherished friend. Between true friends, there can be no conspiracy to do wrong. Friends are to be allies in probity, not profit. Cicero makes the point that the life of the very rich or of the despot is characterized by suspicion about the motive for any apparently friendly act, and that the more equal friends are, the more valid their relationship should be. According to Cicero, friendship was not to be offered on the spur of the moment; evaluation should precede esteem, and flattery should be recognized.

From these brief summaries of Cicero's sentiments, you will correctly surmise that friendship for the Greeks and Romans was a serious matter and in no way equivalent to our current idea of cordial acquaintance. Friendship was an important social bond and buffer. Plutarch approached the matter in an essay called "On the Overabundance of Friends" from a different perspective but with the same message. He tells us that a meaningful relationship with a large number of people is not possible, and that friendship is not a casual characteristic of a herd of cattle or a throng of people, but should be a meaningful relationship between two individuals. He goes on in a passage, which for me has a striking and memorable simile.

> Those observing the large mob and clamor of guests who pass salutations, put out their right hands, or act as protectors, in the dwellings of the rich and powerful, would think them blessed with such an abundance of friends. Yet they see more flies in their kitchens. However, the flies that do not leave the kitchen treats untouched, and the guests who do not leave any benefit untouched, do not remain. To the contrary, real friendship searches for three things most of all: goodness as noble, congeniality as sweetly enjoyable, benefits as obligatory. For one ought to select with discrimination, enjoy associating, and be helpful when needed. These points oppose the overabundance of friends, and especially the most decisive is careful selection. One must consider first if it is possible in a short time to scrutinize choral dancers joining together in the dance, rowers rowing together, household menials entrusted with property, or those who will be escorts for boys, much less very many friends together taking off their clothes for the conflict of every kind of fortune . . .

Plutarch means that they are taking their clothes off as though for an athletic contest. I can never forget the image of a host of false friends feasting on what favors you may have to offer just like a multitude of flies on your groceries. The Greeks and the Romans knew that a friend who liked you only for what he could get out of you was not a friend in any true sense of the word. I have come to suspect that it is easier to see other people being "used" than to apply such understanding for one's self. President Grant did notice that he was not offered fine dinners as often after he was out of office, but that observation might not have required much insight. The role of friendship in our society in which the individual often undergoes changes in income and locale is hard to define, but I think still can be beneficial. Again here we are skirting on differences between the material and the abstract or human. When one selects a friend, is he valued for his character or his material goods? We know how Plutarch or Cicero would choose, but our decision may be problematic in a society in which the emphasis is often on financial success.

SENECA, THE ELDER

ON THE YOUTH OF TODAY

I will describe Seneca's extraordinary memory in chapter V. He seems to have been well to do and probably lived from about 50 B.C. to around A.D 40. We have about half of his composition, which was written in his extreme old age and in which he recalled the speeches as well as characters of famous declaimers he had heard many years previously. Mixed in are interesting historical tidbits and gossip. Some of the selections in his collection are quite moving and others are too artificial for my and probably most contemporary taste. Some of his introductions to the different surviving books show considerable wit and are instructive in an entertaining style. For me he is at his best when he expresses his own rather severe opinions. Towards the beginning of the preface to his first book, although he is actually discussing eloquence and the study of public speaking, he launches into a tirade about the defects of the young men of his time. To some of us, remembering family encounters or other senior commentary, the lecture may sound familiar, but I think it is a wonderful rant.

> . . . From then on, the matter has daily turned to the worse. Whether the cause might be the excess luxury of the times (for nothing is so lethal for mental talent as luxury) or, possibly. since the value of our eloquence has fallen, all competition has been transferred to dishonorable activities which are thriving amid much approba-

tion and money-making. An alternate cause may be that certain fate whose evil and eternal law in all things requires that which has been brought to the highest point slides back to the bottom, in fact more quickly than it had ascended.

See! The mental talents of our lazy youth are numb! They are not awake for the effort of any single decent activity. Sleep and inertia, and what is worse than sleep and inertia, diligent effort in evil business have seized their minds. A lewd enthusiasm for singing and dancing possesses these womanish men. The norm for our young men is to have their hair done, to thin their voice out to feminine endearments, to compete with women in delicacy of physique, and to adorn themselves with the foulest affectations. Who may I say of your peers is creative enough, works enough, no really is a man enough? They stay soft and weak in life the way they were born, while violating the chaste virtue of others, and forgetful of their own. . .

POLYBIUS

THE NATURE OF POLITICAL CHANGE

Polybius was a Greek from a politically prominent family; he was probably born around 200 B.C. in a city called Megalopolis in the district of Greece called Arcadia, and had a sophisticated education. Early in his career, he was the ambassador to Rome of an organization of Greek cities called the Achaean League. He was also ambassador to Egypt, had a military command for the League, and later he was also a senior executive of the League. Although he had not been an opponent of the Romans, after the defeat of King Perseus of Macedonia in 168 B.C, Polybius was one of a thousand leading citizens who were taken to Italy for detention. Although he spent sixteen years in Rome essentially as a political prisoner, he was allowed to stay at the home of one Lucius Aemilus Paulus, the Roman commander who had defeated Perseus and with whom Polybius had previously formed a relationship. (It is interesting to me that this Aemilus beat the Macedonian army and its phalanx formation with which Alexander had conquered the Persian Empire.) Aemilius had two surviving sons and the talented Polybius shared in their education and preparation for public life. He developed a lasting friendship with the younger boy who was adopted (a common and formal familial social maneuver among the Romans to preserve aristocratic patrician families) by the son of Scipio Africanus, the man who had finally defeated the brilliant Hannibal in the long drawn out agony of the second great war with Carthage. The adopted boy became the famous and amazingly capable Scipio Aemilianus.

Like some of the other authors we will review, Polybius was experienced in diplomacy, public life, politics and war. He had many experiences; one of the most dramatic was his presence when his friend Scipio Aemilianus was in command at the defeat and final total destruction of Carthage. He noted that in the short space of about fifty years the Greek and Mediterranean world had come under the total control of Rome. This development was truly phenomenal for those who had observed varying balances of power and advantages swaying to and fro for many years after the death of Alexander and the fragmentation of his empire into large components. Polybius set out to report as truthfully as possible what actually happened and to analyze the causes. He developed theories based on the most careful examination possible. He went to great lengths to get the actual facts of what had happened and then applied his training, experience and intelligence to explain to the Greek world the events and the reasons for them. He spent much time describing the qualities of the Romans, and among these he described their political system that he considered the reason for their success.

Polybius thought that in general, and in the particular case of the Roman state, a people's success or failure should be attributed to the form and quality of their constitutional arrangements. Following previous Greek theory, he noted three basic forms of government: a kingdom, the rule of the best, and democracy or rule by the general body of citizens. He believed that, although each of these forms was initially benign, there was a natural progression and deterioration. Kingdoms evolved into tyrannies, and the rule of the best, or aristocracies, into oligarchies. Here is Polybius' description of what happens after oligarchs are overthrown by a state's citizens.

> . . . Only their faith in themselves remained intact; they made their choice, and out of an oligarchy they turned the political system into a democracy. They themselves undertook the management of common issues with shared good faith. As far as some were still alive of those who had suffered arrogance and power, they welcomed the new constitution and valued freedom of speech and openness to the maximum. When young people are born later and the democracy has been handed down to the children of the children, some desire ascendancy, are no longer so concerned with freedom of speech and equality, and endeavor to have more than anybody else. This tendency is greatest in those who surpass others in riches. Further, whenever they start to lust for power, and they do not have enough skill or merit, they waste away their own wealth, as they entice and debase the multitude by every available means. Consequently, once they have suborned the population into taking presents, and, being greedy for more presents for the sake of a senseless thirst to be popular, then democracy is destroyed and is converted into brute force and physical control. After the citizenry have become habituated to consuming what is another's and have based their expectations for support on the resources of their neighbors, when they get hold of a perceptive and courageous party leader who has been excluded from the honors of government administration because of poverty, then they resort to physical force, they gather together, murder,

> exile citizens, and confiscate land, until they become totally uncivilized and again become subject to a tyrant or a king. This is exactly how systems of government alternate, and is the natural order's management system, as the components of political structures turn, undergo change and again return back into themselves. While anyone having observed these things clearly may be incorrect in predicting the time-frame of future events involving political systems, he still would seldom be wrong about such change or decay and how each may progress, unless he is biased by animosity or envy. However, it is about the Roman political system that this concept will explain how it was constructed, its growth and its prime of life, and likewise its deterioration to come . . .

We should remember at this point that when Polybius speaks of the Roman state, he is not talking about mythology but a polity of determined people who, unlike anyone since, ruled the whole territory around the Mediterranean from Spain to Syria. This achievement was accomplished without any motors, telegraph, firearms or other modern devices.

Now Polybius, although very smart, was not only an academic. He was well-educated, but he speaks about abstract political concepts from a background in active public affairs. Like others to whom I introduce you in these pages, he dealt with real crises and dangers that were both personal as well as political. You will see that some of the others even met political deaths. Comments arising from such a source may be worthy of our attention. I will not compare them here with the writings of those whose sole profession it may be to produce such comments, but Polybius himself does have an interesting remark. He says that to compare the constitution of actual states with Plato's Republic is just like comparing a living man with a statue.

What Polybius does seem to like among political systems (and the idea is not original with him) is a balanced or mixed constitution composed of all three basic elements, which are again: kingship, the rule of the best, and democracy. He describes in detail and praises the Roman system of government with its consuls, senate and people essentially forming a system of checks and balances. Our "founding fathers" were familiar with the work of Polybius and quoted him during the debates at the constitutional convention in 1787. He is at least one source for the separation of powers enshrined in our federal constitution. To continue, Polybius did not think that a system such as that of the Romans was immune to the natural process of deterioration, and predicted accurately the downfall of the Roman republic, which, of course, did occur a hundred or so years later, after decades of considerable violence, tumult and blood. At this point, I always have a chilling thought. If Polybius were alive today and were observing the evolution of our American republic, what would he predict for us? You may remember Franklin's response when he was asked what kind of government the constitutional convention had created: "A republic if you can keep it."

VALERIUS MAXIMUS

ON MEMORABLE OLD AGE

In antiquity, as now, those who reached extreme age, and who were productive at their advanced years, were very much the subject of interest and admiration. Much surviving literature contains fine stories and anecdotes about mature years, and especially in the pages of Plutarch and Cicero, analyses of the meaning and value of old age. The latter identifies supposedly negative qualities of old age that are usually thought to be burdensome, and elegantly demonstrates that they are indeed benefits. He holds that the finer pursuits of seniority do not require a young man's strength, and that less desire for physical pleasures frees the mind for clearer thought. Death is a risk at any age and is a natural process. I am not able to summarize more of Cicero's presentation adequately without diminishing and distorting its quality, and his *On Old Age* is well worth reading in its entirety for its art as well as its philosophy. All ancient commentaries are united in their admiration of successful and meaningful old age. Sometimes such individuals are glorified and held up as idols, concepts that may seem strange to our youth-oriented society. However, in the practice of urology one meets so very many gray-haired men and women who are clever, cheerful, capable, experienced - possessing all these qualities and more. I would say that in my office such people were the norm. There was Martha, who remembered standing up in her child's bed in 1898 and being afraid that the Spanish were going to get her, but whose taste in clothes was simply the best of any woman I have ever met and whose comments on human relations were unequaled when she was just short of one hundred. There is my current friend Anna, who at a hundred and two years of age remembers Theodore Roosevelt campaigning in 1912 in an open touring car festooned with American flags, and who writes lucid and instructive prose and is an acute historian.

I am going to show you a description of a famous ancient because he reminds me of an actual person of my local community. His name is Masinissa and a nice, if not original, description of him may be found in the pages of Valerius Maximus, whose nine books of dramatic selections *On Memorable Deeds and Statements* were written under the emperor Tiberius after A.D. 31. The work is a compendium of various Roman and Greek examples in various categories such as: omens, dreams, military discipline, bravery, friendship, poverty, mercy, ingratitude, severity, justice, fidelity, wisdom and cleverness, character, famous wills and trials, the power of eloquence, glory, luxury, cruelty, anger, hatred, greed, human error, revenge, and famous deaths. This approach written in an age lacking trained sociologists and psychiatrists was interesting to me, and I spent much time with this author in my evenings. Although he can be pompous, sententious and moralizing, his Latinity is easy and pleasant, he concentrates remarkable stories in one place, and occasionally he is the only source for some interesting material. To return to the man whose description by Valerius Maximus we have selected, Masinissa was a renowned ally of the Romans in the great war with Hannibal. He lived from 238 to 148 B.C. and began his career - he excelled as a commander of cavalry - in support of the Carthaginians and then switched sides and was steadfastly loyal to the Romans. He experienced great extremes of fortune, at times was isolated on the losing side, but ended as the acknowledged king of Numidia. He was even involved in a famous love triangle with a Carthaginian princess who was the wife of his chief rival. He was fearless, capable, strong and wily, and managed to avoid being crushed between the huge forces of Rome and Carthage. There is probably some considerable accuracy in the following sketch.

> . . . Masinissa, king of Numidia, experienced a reign of sixty years, and also achieved more respect than all men for his hardy old age. It is certain that he, in just the manner that Cicero reports in the book which he wrote about old age, could never be convinced to protect his head with a covering in any cold or rain. They also say that it was this same individual's habit to remain standing where he had placed his feet for some hours, not moving a toe before he had worn out the young men around him who were trying to do the same thing. And also, if he had any duties to perform while sitting down, he always stayed on his throne and did not reposition his body at all. In fact, he usually led his armies around the clock while continuously on horseback. In no respect did he discontinue any of the activities, which he had been used to doing as a young man, in order to make his old age more comfortable. He also even had such vigor in the exercises of Venus that after he was eighty-six he fathered a son who was named Methymnus. And through his continued efforts in agriculture, he left the empty and abandoned territory that he had taken over in a fruitful condition.

This description of Masinissa's active old age reminded me of the reports that a patient years ago gave me about his centenarian father. His work was not military or political, but in horticulture, yet he too tilled actively and went about our community at an advanced age, lightly clothed and bareheaded, with his prized and sought-after agricultural products. He too, being a widower for a number of years, was presented with a much younger bride "from the old country" and became a father again well in his eighties. The word "king" was used as part of an admiring sobriquet by which he was known. Certainly, he was a man to be respected if not emulated.

There were many stories of extreme old age in ancient times, some possible and probable, and others clearly fictitious. Currently in clinical and office medical practice one meets many wonderful and inspiring individuals, remarkable for who they are regardless of advanced age. I remember the oldest patient that I have seen. Early in my training, we made house calls in the Boston area in a carefully supervised program. This opportunity was very satisfying because there was at last a chance, even though limited, to help. On one occasion, I was called to see a teenaged girl who complained of a sore throat. I examined her carefully and cultured her throat. If a streptococcal infection had been proven, she would have then received a prescription for an appropriate course of antibiotics. I explained the plan to her and prepared to leave, and she said, "While you're here, why don't you check Grandma Bertie?" I agreed and she took me into a back bedroom where there was a very large bed with a very small African-American woman in it. The woman looked old and I whispered to my first patient, "How old is she?" She answered, "We don't know for sure, we think she's one hundred and fifteen, but slaves didn't have birth certificates." I swallowed and went over to examine the elderly lady. She had sparse gray hair, her skin showed a pattern of fine wrinkles, and she had large lustrous brown eyes. I listened to her heart and lungs, checked her blood pressure, but all the time I knew that my poor skills, let alone that of any other physician, had little to offer a person of such awesome seniority. Everything seemed to be quite in order. I then engaged her in conversation. Her hearing was good, and she had a deep melodious voice without any marked accent. She indeed recalled being a slave as a little girl, but then, and I thought that there was still a note of surprise in her tone, she said that, "The blue soldiers came, and the white folks ran away and I was free!" I was talking with someone who had seen the Union army in action and had benefited directly. It was an overwhelming experience for me; she was smiling when I left.

I recall another impressive patient also related to the same period in history. At another stage in my training, we rotated to evaluate patients in a facility that provided support services for the elderly. I was struck in particular by one man whose mental capacity was more than intact, although he was physically disabled and required help for personal care. I remember that he had carefully combed white hair and bright blue eyes. He was disgruntled when I first met him, and I found out that he did not feel that he was treated with adequate respect by some of the staff and that some of the details in his daily care were inappropriate. For some reason I found him very attractive and interesting, and did my best to correct some of his problems. When I had time, I would spend free moments in conversation with him and try on a variety of subjects to solicit his opinions, which often had value and insight. We seemed to hit it off well and under other circumstances might have been friends. All too soon, my time on that rotation came to an end and I went to him to say goodbye. He said that I had treated him well and that he was grateful and that he wanted to shake my hand. I said, and meant it, that I had been very happy to know him and to try to help. He then told me a short tale. It seemed that when he was very young (remember he was well over a hundred when I knew him) that his father had been involved in politics. His father and mother took him to the national capitol during a presidential campaign. He was very young but he remembered seeing a very tall man with a very tall hat. His mother told him later when he was a little older that he had been taken to see the president who was running for a second term. The president offered to kiss him, and his mother demurred saying that he was a little man now and that the president should shake his hand, and he did so. Now my patient said as he took my hand, "You have done a lot for me and I can't do much for you, but now you know that you have shaken hands with a man who shook hands with Lincoln." He also told me that if I should know a worthy person that I should pass it on, and I have done that.

Chapter V

THE POET'S VIEW

Another source to tell us about ourselves lies in the art of poets. Their themes are uniquely human, and communicate most easily across the boundaries of time, language and culture, often by evoking common emotional experience. I have picked three broad categories in the following selections. The first three, deceptively simple but quite polished, deal with birds and loss, the fourth and fifth with rural life and the last two are by two female authors, one more famous than the other, but both immediate and personal. A very kind fortune has preserved these for us.

CALLIMACHUS

THE NIGHTINGALES OF HERACLEITUS

The exact dates of Callimachus' birth and death are unknown but reasonable estimates are 310 and 235 B.C. He was a sophisticated and polished writer in the Hellenistic kingdom of Egypt under King Ptolemy II, the son of Alexander's friend and subordinate commander who had founded the dynasty. Once again, there are limited sources of information about the life of this author. We are told that he wrote an unbelievable eight hundred books, and he was certainly known in antiquity as a scholar and librarian (not chief librarian) in the great library at Alexandria; we tend to think of him now as a poet. The passage of centuries have left us from his writings only six hymns (to

Zeus, Apollo, Artemis, the island of Delos, Athena, Demeter) and sixty-four epigrams as well as various bits and fragments. One passage of fourteen lines describes the violation of Simonides' tomb without any fear of retribution by Castor and Pollux, Simonides' divine protectors at the banquet of Scopas which you have read about in chapter 2. Callimachus was popular with those who came after him, especially the Romans, and we have one of his lost works translated into Latin by the poet Catullus (more of whom shortly).

There was a famous heated dispute between Callimachus and his student and later competitor, Apollonius. Callimachus supported shorter, often learned, more "modern" literature versus Apollonius' longer, more romantic, traditional and epic style. Interestingly almost six thousand lines of Apollonius' work survives in fifty-two manuscripts and many papyrus fragments. This work of Apollonius, called the *Argonautica,* comprises greater amount of material than that which we have for Callimachus. There is a famous remark attributed to Callimachus: "a big book, a big evil", and in a surviving fragment he does say that when he was young Apollo told him "to maintain a slender muse". I should add that more recent scholarship has questioned the whole story of the quarrel, as entertaining as it may be.

I have picked an epigram that survives in a quotation by a later biographer of philosophers. The Heracleitus addressed here is not the famous philosopher of 500 B.C. who taught us that one cannot put his foot in the same river twice, but a poet-friend of Callimachus who lived in the noble city of Halicarnassus, where stood the great tomb called the Mausoleum, one of the seven wonders of the ancient world.

Someone spoke of your fate, O Heracleitus,
And brought me to tears.
I was reminded how often the both of us conversed
  together
And made the sun set.
But still your ashes are four-fold ancient,
O guest-friend from Halicarnassus.
On the other hand, your nightingales live on.
Hades that snatches everything lays not a hand on them.

CATULLUS

LESBIA'S SPARROW

Catullus' dates are probably 84 to 54 B.C. He was born in Verona and it was in Verona in the early years of the fourteenth century that a single manuscript was somehow found "under a bushel." This manuscript was then lost, but not before at least three copies had been made and he escaped the eternal darkness. He did die young, and left us a very slim volume of only 114 poems. However, they are a vital and amazing collection. There is a wide range of subject and style: epic hexameters about mythological stories, hymns, delicate, sincere verses on love, graphic insults and sexual threats, all versatile and original even when overt copies of Greek precursors. There are four hundred impressive lines on the marriage of Peleus and Thetis, the parents of Achilles, a wonderful marriage song apparently written for friends, short insults, and the short pieces, for which he is most famous, verses to Lesbia, the flawed object of his affection, at first full of love and then despair. For example, one of his poems states that he loves and hates (Lesbia, of course) at the same time, which forms the best short expression that I know describing what psychiatrists tell us are not uncommon mixed feelings. In the intensity of his emotion, he is definitely a Latin writer, but his style is influenced by the Greek authors of the Hellenistic period, after the death of Alexander in 323 B.C.

To give you a frame of reference, Julius Caesar was assassinated on March 15, 44 B.C. (the famous Ides of March). To me there has always seemed to be a great difference between the freewheeling extremes of Catullus and the polished orthodoxy of the next generation of poets. How much of this perceived difference may be due to the establishment of stable one-man rule under the emperor Augustus and the loss of the freedoms of the fallen Roman republic, or just to the artistry of Catullus and the evolution of poetic taste or fashion, I will leave to others to decide.

In such a versatile and ingenious text, it is hard to decide on a selection, especially considering the vagaries of contemporary taste, but with a writer like Catullus, sometimes well-known pieces are still fresh and readable. Here I intend to offer something that you may have seen or heard about previously. I read these over fifty years ago, but I am still charmed by them.

Sparrow, darling of my girl friend
She loves to play with you,
To hold you up to her bosom,
To hold out her finger-tip to your attack
And encourage your sharp pecks.
I would think that when she, my shining desire,
Favors some such endearing game
You could be some small relief for her anguish
And assuage the intensity of her passion.
Would that I could play with you the way that she does
And alleviate the melancholy anxiety in my own mind.

Unfortunately, there is not a happy ending for the little bird as we see in the next poem. The delicacy of feeling continues however.

Grieve, O Love and Cupids,
And as many elegant men as possible.
My girl-friend's sparrow is dead,
My girl-friend's sparrow, her darling,
Whom she used to love more than her own eyes,
For he was sweet as honey and
In addition, recognized her the way a girl knows her own
mother.
He did not budge from her lap,
But jumping about now here, now there,
Was ever peeping to his lady-lord alone.
He now travels that dark road
To the place from which they deny that anyone returns.
May it be ill for you, O evil darkness of the underworld
That gulps down everything beautiful,
Such a beautiful sparrow have you carried off!

The imagination of a modern painter shows us Lesbia and her sparrow.

O evil deed! O poor little sparrow!
For your sake my girl-friend's eyes
Are delicately swollen and red with weeping.

In recent years uncensored translations of Catullus have been published which present the full range of his remarkable talent. Here I again step beyond my self imposed boundaries and advise the reader to look further into his remarkable work which is full of vitality.

OVID

CORINNA'S PARROT

Ovid was born in 43 B.C., the year that Cicero was murdered, about ninety miles east of Rome. He was well educated at Rome and at Athens and much of his work has survived. He wrote poetry about love in a variety of books, about mythology and transformations of humans into other forms, and lastly sad verses from his place of exile and death in A.D. 18 on the coast of the Black Sea.

He was very skillful in poetry, which he implied came naturally to him, and to me his use of the Latin language shows exceptional virtuosity. His three books of love elegies are well thought of and from them I have selected another bird-poem. You will notice that in these lines he shows off his learning, but ends up with something that reminds of us of today's pet cemeteries. I find this very different from the offering of Catullus, indeed almost artificial, but there is an element of parody here, as well. He was writing for a rich, well read, I suspect sometimes bored, public that was the elite of the rulers of the known world. He dramatizes the death of a pet bird, refers to obscure mythological characters (I have simplified some of the references, believe it or not), follows the forms of respect for a departed human contemporary, portrays an underworld for virtuous birds rather than men, and finally constructs a cleverly phrased tombstone inscription. This all seems to add up to a pose, rather than sincerity or universality, but it is artfully done.

The details of his girldriend Corinna's bird seem to represent a description of a green Indian ring-neck parrot, which is still a common pet today, said to be very sociable, and can be taught to talk—English as well as Latin. After Augustus defeated Antony and Cleopatra, and Egypt came under Roman rule, there was increased trade with the east. The writer Strabo tells us that during the time of Augustus one hundred and twenty vessels a year sailed for India. Many Roman coin hoards have been found in India. A travel document of the first century of our era describes in considerable detail maritime trade routes from Egypt to the coast of India. Even the east coast of India and the Ganges River are included. There is also an historical record of an Indian king sending an ambassador to Augustus.

I must add here a few words about some of Ovid's mythological references. Philomela, whose rape by her Thracian brother-in-law was avenged by another atrocity, the dismemberment and serving up of her nephew Itys to the rapist, was according to Ovid's writing elsewhere turned into a nightingale. This family may be mythological, but is clearly very dysfunctional. Pylades was the very close friend and supporter of Orestes who was pursued by the Furies after he killed his mother Clytemnestra and her boy-friend Aegisthus, who for his part had murdered Agamemnon when he finally returned from defeating the Trojans. Thersites was said to be very ugly and to have seen the funeral of the first to die in the Trojan War, in which Hector died later and more famously at the hands of Achilles. These kinds of learned references followed the style of previous writers and probably added some mood or atmosphere. In our age, there may be no strict comparison, but biblical references in some kinds of writing might be comparable.

The Parrot, mimic bird from India of the dawn, perished.
Gather O birds to his funeral!
Gather O virtuous fliers; beat your breasts with your feathers!
Scratch your soft cheeks with hard claw!
Let your plumage be unkempt and torn like hair in mourning,
And let your songs sound forth like the great trumpet!
O Philomela, your squawking about the sin of the Thracian tyrant
Has been satisfied in full by the passage of time.
Turn to attend the pitiful last rites of a rare bird;
Itys is a great but ancient reason for anguish.
All of you who balance your flights in the fluid air,
Especially you, turtledove, before all others, mourn!
You two birds filled your life with perfect harmony

And your enduring and constant fidelity persisted to the end.
What young Pylades was to Grecian Orestes
So was the turtle dove to you, parrot, as long as it was permitted.
But what good was such fidelity? Or a body of uncommon hue?
Or your voice gifted in varying sound?
What good was it that you delighted my girl-friend when she got you?
Splendor of birds, you definitely lie dead, out of luck.
Your feathers could make emerald look pale and dim.
You had a purple-red beak washed in scarlet saffron.
You reproduced sound so well with your croaking
That no bird in the world could imitate speech better.
Envy carried you off - you were not a fighter.
You were verbose and loved peace and quiet.
See! Quail live on amid their battles,
Maybe that is the reason many of them get old.
You were filled with a tiny nibble.
Your love of conversation let you keep your mouth empty amid many treats.
A nut was your meal, and poppy put you to sleep,
And the moisture of plain water dispelled your thirst,
The greedy vulture lives on,
And the hawk drawing circles through the air,
And the jackdaw that produces rain,
And lives the crow that Minerva, who bears arms, despises,
And that even has nine lives.
But that talkative likeness of the human voice perished
The parrot, a present given from the far ends of the earth!

The best are nearly always the first to be carried off by greedy hands;
The lesser complete their number of years.
Thersites saw the sad funeral of Protesliaus
And Hector was ash at the time when his brothers still lived.
Why should I relate my frightened girl friend's prayers on your behalf?
Prayers that were blown out over the sea by the stormy south wind.
Came the seventh day which was not going to be followed by another,
And one of the Fates stood before you with a spindle from which the thread had run out.
But not even then were the words in your listless throat numbed.
Dying your tongue called out "Farewell, Corinna!"
Near the high ground in heaven a wood is leafy with dark oak trees
And the damp soil is green with eternal grass.
If there is any faith in the unknown, that is called the place of the virtuous fliers,
From which all bad birds are kept away.
There far and wide swans feed safely
As well as the phoenix that lives forever, always just a single bird.
Juno's peacock fans out his feathers,
The caressing dove kisses her eager male mate.
The parrot has been accepted among them in the sylvan home
And has the virtuous birds paying attention to his words.

A monument mound covers his bones, a mound very
large for his body,
On which a small stone appropriate for him has an epigram:
"By this tomb I am deemed to have pleased my mistress.
And to have had a mouth learned in speech more than a
bird.

VIRGIL

THE COUNTRY LIFE

I first read Virgil's *Aeneid* at the age of sixteen at my school. Later I read his other works and he stayed with me during my days of doing surgery. Although now my taste is perhaps more mature and my experience of life is certainly wider, I still approach him with a combination of awe and intimacy. Now that may seem strange, but anyone who knows his artistry and universality will recognize my feelings at once.

So who was Virgil? He appears to have been a gifted country boy from near Mantua in Northern Italy who was given a refined education by his father. His early manhood was affected by the disruptions, murders, civil wars, and confiscations that accompanied the demise of the Roman republic in the first century B.C. His personal future was assured by contact with the highest level of contemporary authority, but I have always thought that his gentle melancholy was forged by the political conflicts around him. Contrary to traditional opinion, his soulful face has survived, depicted in many double portraits in which he is combined with Homer. It is a wonderful visage.

Many have read, or at least heard of, the *Aeneid.* The traditional story holds that Virgil worked on the poem for many years but that it was unfinished when during his final illness he asked that it be burned. It appears to have been edited by others post mortem, and then published. There is some evidence in our text that Virgil did not finish his work. There are fifty-five incomplete lines, and other verses that seem inconclusive or imperfect. He did have time to bring to perfection his other two earlier works, the *Eclogues* and the *Georgics*. The *Eclogues* comprise ten short poems of a hundred lines each more or less, and depict an idealized pastoral setting. The *Georgics*, in four books of mostly over five hundred lines each, follow the ancient tradition of didactic poetry. The first book describes raising crops, the second the culture of trees, the third the care of agricultural animals, and the fourth bee-keeping. The work, in my opinion, contains the most skilled and polished, not to say moving and sublime, poetic composition in Latin. I still remember vividly the first time that I read the following lines and how I then concluded that all the effort I had expended previously to learn the Latin language was made worthwhile by the experience. I append my humble attempt at translation, but I will remind the gentle reader that neither I nor anyone can reproduce Virgil's music in English. This passage is from the end of book II.

> O farmers! Too fortunate if they should know their own blessings!
> For them the earth herself, so very equitable, pours out from the soil
> A ready support far away from the conflict of weapons.
> Even if early in the morning an exalted home
> With vainglorious foyers does not regurgitate
> An enormous wave of callers paying respects from the whole residence,
> Or they do not gaze open-mouthed at beautiful doors of tortoise-shell ornamentation,
> And at garments elaborated with gold, and Corinthian bronzes,
> Or Assyrian dye does not color the white wool,
> Or flower perfume for ointment does not spoil the benefit of olive oil:
> Yet still they have untroubled rest and a life unacquainted with deceit,
> And rich in different resources. Also relaxation in broad estates,

Grottoes and lakes that are alive; also cool valleys,
And the lowing of cows, and sweet sleep under a tree.
There are the glens and the lairs of beasts,
And a youth that tolerates labor and is accustomed to scarcity,
And the observances of the gods and parents held sacred.
Among them as Justice departed from the earth, she set her final footprints.
May the sweet Muses, whose holy objects I bear,
Smitten with immense love, receive me first above all things, and
In addition, make known the pathways of heaven and the constellations,
The different fadings of the sun and the labors of the moon;
Whence comes the earthquake; what force makes the deep sea
Break its bonds, swell, and then sink down into itself again;
Why the wintry sun hurries so much to bathe in the ocean,
Or what delay hinders the unhurried nights.
If however, the blood around my heart is cold and hinders me
So that I may be unable to come near these components of nature,
May I be happy with the countryside and rivers that water the valleys.
Even without fame may I love the streams and the woods.
O where are the fields and Spercheos and Taygeta
Where the Spartan maids do Bacchic revel?
O, who will put me in the cool valleys of Haemus

And shelter me with the great shade of the branches there?
Fortunate he who was able to know the reasons for things,
And hurl under his feet all fear and inescapable destiny
And the reverberation of greedy Acheron.
And fortunate he who knew the rural gods
And Pan and old Silvanus and the nymphs, all sisters.
Neither the symbols of authority of the people, nor the purple of kings
Deflected him and not conflict inciting disloyal brothers
And not the Dacians coming down from the Danube River
Where they swear for success together, and
Not the affairs of Rome and kingdoms that will perish.
He did not feel sorry for and pity one without means, or envy a possessor;
He plucked the fruits which the branches, which the willing countryside
Have born of their own will, nor did he observe laws of iron
And the mad forum or the record hall of the people.
Others agitate unknown seas with their oars and run onto sword iron,
And make their way into the forecourts and entrances of kings.
This one seeks out a city and the pitiable gods of each home for destruction
So that he might drink from a goblet of precious stone and sleep on Tyrian purple.
Another collects riches and sits over hidden, buried gold.
That one is dumbfounded, stunned by the speaking platform.

The applause of the commons and the senators redoubled along the rows of seats
Grips someone else with his mouth open.
Drenched in the blood of brothers, they are delighted,
And they exchange their homes and sweet thresholds for exile
And pursue a native land that lies under another sun.
The farmer parts the ground with his curved plow.
From this is the year's work, from this he supports his native land, small descendants,
From this his herds of cattle and deserving oxen.
There is no stopping without the year abounding in fruits or with the young of the flocks
Or with the sheaf of grain-stalk and loading the furrows with the harvest
And overwhelming the barns. Winter comes. The olive is ground in the press,
The hogs return delighted with acorn; the woods provide wild strawberries,
And autumn sets out a variety of bearings,
And on high, the ripe vintage is warmed on the sunny rocks.
Between times his sweet children hang on his kisses,
His pure home guards its modesty, the cows hang teats full of milk,
And fat young goats contend horn to horn on the happy grass.
He himself observes the holidays, stretches out on the grass
Where around the fire in the middle
His associates circle garlands around their wine bowl;
Pouring a libation, he calls on you O Bacchus
And for the chief herders sets up on the elm the contest for the swift javelin,

And they undress their rugged bodies for the rustic
sports field.
At one time, the old Sabine tribe practiced this life, as
did Remus and his brother.
In this way, Etruria assuredly grew valiant
And Rome was made the fairest of all things
And surrounded her seven summits with one wall.
Before the rule of Jupiter and the sinful race fed on slain
young bulls
Golden Saturn fostered this life on earth.
Not as yet had they heard the trumpet's battle signal
Or the screech of a sword laid on the hard forge.

TIBULLUS

WAR AND PEACE AND LOVE

"In the judgment of most he holds the first place among the writers of elegy." So stated the anonymous author of an ancient life of Tibullus. "We also challenge the Greeks in elegiac poetry in which to me Tibullus seems to be the most polished and refined." This was the opinion of Quintilian, a leading teacher in rhetoric and literature; among his students was the younger Pliny whom we have met previously in these pages. Tibullus was probably born about a century earlier than Quintilian, between 55 and 48 B.C. Besides what can be surmised from his writings, we know little about him. It seems that he was quite handsome and careful in his dress and grooming, but there is no image of him that has been recognized. He was a friend of the poets Ovid and Horace; from the latter we learn that Tibullus had a country place about ten miles south of the city of Rome. While Horace's patron was Maecenas, Tibullus' benefactor was Messalla, not the fictional and evil Messalla of the novel *Ben Hur*, but a distinguished and prominent Roman: Marcus Valerius Messalla Corvinus. From this mouthful of a name, you may infer correctly that this man was a member of an old and respected patrician family; in order to support the republic, he had a military command on the side of

Brutus and Cassius, the assassins of Julius Caesar. After the loss at the battle of Philippi, some of the events of which you may remember were dramatized by Shakespeare, Messalla made his peace with the new order and on behalf of the emperor Augustus even won a provincial war in the area near Bordeaux. There was, however, always about him a hint of support for the old free republic. He was also highly admired for his writing none of which survives, and he attracted a coterie of writers among whom the principal was Tibullus. We are told that Tibullus was very close to Messalla, accompanied him as a junior officer, and actually received military decorations during the campaign in what is now southwestern France. He died young in 19 B.C., the same year as did Vergil. Contemporary verses of remembrance have an unjust death sending him to be Vergil's companion in the Elysian Fields.

I find it fascinating that a hundred years and more after his death, Tibullus was considered to be the first among the writers of elegy, and that now many educated individuals have never heard of him. (By elegy, we mean poetry written in a certain kind of verse couplets, which at his time often dealt with the personal and emotional issues of the writer.) Sixteen short poems definitely attributed to him by name survive and, together with a small amount of material from other writers of the literary circle of Messalla, form a slim volume today. Tibullus' verses deal with love for a woman and a boy and are marked by grace and charm; he achieves that deceptive simplicity which is characteristic of high art. His writing is considerably enriched by rural themes, and for me each poem is jewel-like and it is difficult to pick one of them for reproduction here. You can decide whether in our selection the subjects he explores represent a literary posture, reflect his real dislike of his former military service, or imply an awareness of bodily fragility and an illness which was to carry him off at a young age. Love and war do seem to be issues with which we are familiar today. On reflection however, I really cannot think of an era in which we have not had to deal with such things. A close reading generates many implications. I will leave these to you as well.

Who first discovered fear-inspiring swords?
How bestial he was and truly iron!
Then killings, then pitched battles came to pass for mankind.
Then a faster road to terrible death was opened.
Or is it not that poor devil's fault
When we turn what he gave us to use against dangerous wild beasts
To our own evil?
We can blame the richness of gold for this.
There were no wars when wooden drinking cups stood next to the meal.
There were no fortresses, no ramparts,
And the lord of the flock was not anxious when he slept among his skittish sheep.
I should have lived then and I would not have known the somber weapons
Nor heard the trumpet with a palpitating heart.
Now I am dragged to war, and
Even now, some enemy is carrying the spears that will stick in my side.
Even so, keep me safe, O home-gods of my ancestors!
As well, you sustained me when in my childhood
I used to run here and there in front of your feet.
There is no shame in your being made from an old log.
Just so you lodged in the abode of my grandfather of old.
Then they held to their faith better
When the poorly attired wooden god was standing in his little shrine.
He was appeased whether someone had made an offering of grapes
Or had placed a garland of grain on his holy hair,
And someone whose prayers had been fulfilled was carrying cake offerings

And next, his little daughter was carrying immaculate honeycomb.
Nevertheless, O house-gods, keep the bronze spears away from me!

—one or more lines thought to be missing here—

And a pig from a full sty, a rustic sacrifice.
Let me follow it with a clean garment
And carry a basket tied round with myrtle
And I with my head tied round with myrtle.
May you accept me thus.
Let another be brave in arms
And with the favor of Mars strike down hostile chiefs
So that he the soldier may be able to recount his deeds to me as I drink
And paint his campaigns on the table with wine.
What is this insanity to call up black death with wars?
It is near at hand and comes stealthily with silent tread.
Below there are no crops, no cultivated vineyards,
But brutal Cerberus and the repugnant navigator of the waters of the Styx.
There a pale throng with shocked eyes and burnt hair
Wanders by shadowy pools.
In fact he who with his offspring prepared
Is struck down by a lingering old age in his cottage
Should be eulogized all the more.
It is he who pursues the sheep, and his son the lambs,
And his wife heats the water for him when he is wearied.
May I be like that, and may I get to have my head shine with white hair
And to recall what we did in the old days when I am aged.
Meanwhile let peace cultivate the fields.
Radiant peace first led the oxen to plow under the arched yoke.

Peace nourished the vine and stored the juice of the grape
So that the father's bottle might pour out wine for the son.
In peace the hoe and the plow shine while in the shadows
Rust takes hold of the doleful arms of the sturdy soldier.

—probably more lines missing here—

Barely sober, the countryman conveys his wife and children home
From the sacred grove in his cart.
But then the war of love ignites and the ladylove bewails
Her torn hair, and cries over a black eye
But the conqueror weeps that his lunatic hands have been so forceful.
Further, wanton Cupid provides the evil words for the quarrel
And sits unconcerned between the two angry lovers.
Ah, whoever strikes his girl is stone and iron;
He tears the gods down from the heavens!
Let tearing off the delicate cloth from her limbs be enough.
Let mussing her hair be enough.
Let bringing on tears be enough.
Infinitely blessed is he if just vexation is enough to make the girl weep.
But he who is physically abusive should carry shield and army tools
And stay far, far away from tender Venus.
And so kind Peace, come to us,
And bear a sheaf of wheat
And may fruits overflow from the front of your gown.

SAPPHO

SONG TO APHRODITE

Ancient mythology told of nine goddesses, the Muses, who inspired those who produced the creative arts, but Plato and Antipater wrote that they thought that there was a tenth Muse: the poet Sappho. Antipater stated further that in poetry she stood out among women, as did Homer among men. Today that would be like saying she was the equal of Shakespeare or Milton. We might conclude that the destruction of almost all of her nine books of poetry may be our greatest literary loss. Only one possibly complete poem is available, quoted at length by a writer from the time of Augustus Caesar. There are several other large fragments. There was great excitement in recent years when scholars reconstructed a short portion of a complete poem by Sappho about her old age from an early papyrus fragment and a later mummy wrapping.

Our biographical information about Sappho is incomplete or ambiguous. She was probably born in the late seventh century B.C. and in the recently reconstructed poem she complains about being too old to dance; it sounds as though she got old enough to have gray hair. She was born into an upper class family from the towns of Eresus and Mytilene on the island of Lesbos, but at some time in her life was exiled for political reasons to Sicily where there was a famous statue of her in the city of Syracuse until the time of Cicero about five hundred years later. Her contemporary, the poet Alcaeus, described her as having a sweet smile, and we do have an image of her in a statue that is thought to be a Roman copy of a Greek original. There are also several paintings on ancient Greek vases, which depict her holding a lyre. Although we have the words of a few of her songs, we do not have the music and we must imagine or try to reconstruct the sound, but all in antiquity praised her greatly for a wonderfully harmonious choice of words.

Here we see the origin of the term "lyric poetry". What she and others developed were originally songs concerning personal subjects and issues and which were vocalized with the accompaniment of the musical notes of the lyre.

From the fragments of her songs and from the notices about her in ancient literature, we know that Sappho wrote admirably and intimately about love. Nevertheless, some of the contemporary interest in her arises from her apparent direction of that love to other women or girls. At this distance in time and with our very limited historical resources, it is hard to know Sappho's deepest desires. There are reports that she was married and had a beloved daughter, and it is likely that there was extensive gender segregation of unmarried women in her island society with what may have been complex culturally determined relationships between them as a result. However, there are ancient comments about her homoerotic inclination. Was she married, had a daughter and then "came out?" Alternatively, were amatory relations between women before marriage encouraged? Fortunately, since we are not as beset by social prejudices as our Victorian ancestors, we do not have to care about such issues and can appreciate her and her work as a human whole. I should also point out that in antiquity, sexuality was not bound up with religion and sin or even concepts of normality and pathology, and what was considered acceptable sexual behavior was more of an issue of social status.

Sappho wrote in a dialect called Aeolic, which had vowel and case ending differences from the Attic, the form of ancient Greek commonly studied. So little of Sappho remains and it is so popular that there is extensive study of her texts; there is much annotation and explanation to help in translation. The small number of pieces longer than single line fragments also helps in the selection process, and I have picked the longest which, as I have previously stated, is quoted at length and which many believe to be complete. In going through her work to prepare this chapter I was again so impressed that I can only apply to her one of her own famous phrases: "more golden than gold".

O immortal Aphrodite, on your ornamented throne,
Daughter of Zeus, who intertwines guileful plans, I beg you,
Noble lady, do not overwhelm my spirit with aggravation and grief.

But come here, and, if once at another time hearing my voice from afar
You listened, and leaving the golden house of your father, you came,
Having yoked your chariot, when,
Quickly flapping their wings, beautiful sparrows carried you
Over the dark earth away from heaven through the mid-air,
And arrived quickly. And you, o blissful one,
Smiling on me with your immortal face,
Asked what was my problem again,
And why did I summon you again,
And again in my maddened heart what I wanted to happen to me:
"And who do I persuade again to return to your affection?
Who does you wrong, O Sappho?
And if she runs away from you, suddenly she will pursue you.
If she refuses gifts, on the contrary she will bestow them
If she does not love you, quickly she will love you, even not willingly."
Come to me right now, relieve my painful anxieties,
Provide me with the degree of fulfillment that my soul desires,
And you yourself be my ally.

This song has been considered to be complete, but I have always felt that we break off in the midst of Sappho's requests to the goddess. Since Sappho was an ancient, I wonder if it would not be natural for her to go on and offer something in return to Aphrodite. Perhaps to place garlands on her altar, or at least feed some sparrows which were to a degree sacred to the goddess. I would have thought that if she wanted something from her favorite divinity, and not, it seems, for the first time, in those days she would promise something in return. Nevertheless, the verses as they stand are certainly marvelously explicit about the uncertain anxieties of passion and love. Her use of language is untranslatable.

SULPICIA

GENUINE ARDOR

We have met Tibullus, the star of the circle of Messalla. His manuscripts include poems by other authors. One of these authors was probably a young woman who called herself Sulpicia, but we can see from her words that her real name was Servia. Names such as Corinna or Lesbia, which we have seen in the poetry of other writers of love elegy, are taken from mythology or history and used as pseudonyms for the identity of real women. There has been much scholarly interest in these six poems recently with a broad range of opinions, some feminist and others going so far as to assert that she did not exist and was a fiction perpetrated by Tibullus or another male colleague. To a degree, I suspect that some of the arguments reflect our own current cultural concerns. Be that as it may, the traditional position is that she was the niece or close relative of Marcus Valerius Messalla Corvinus, and was probably his ward. We have no real biographical information about her beyond what is implied in the poetry, but my impression when reading about her intensity, her complaints and enthusiasms, is of a quite young, perhaps teen-aged, woman. I am greatly impressed by her skill at saying so much of a subtle nature in so few words. Some of her fervor and drama seems quite familiar in the realm of young love. One also often sees the comment that she is the only woman poet from antiquity whose verses are intact and not fragments. You can decide for yourself how feminine and familiar her sentiments may be.

In the third line that follows below the adjective "Cytherean" refers to an island off the coast of Greece sacred to the goddess of love.

Finally comes love, the kind that I would have been
More embarrassed to hide than expose.

Cytherean Venus was persuaded by my Roman muses;
She brought him and put him in my embrace.
She has performed as promised; let her tell of my rapture
Should anybody miss such joy for herself.
I would not wish to commit anything to signed letters
In case someone reads them before he who is mine does.
I am delighted that I was naughty.
It's a bore to arrange a fabricated expression.
Let the story be that I was fit for him and he was fit for
me.

Here comes my odious birthday.
It's going to be a sad celebration
In the nasty country, and without my Cerinthus.
What is more delightful than the city?
Is a country house more suitable for a girl,
Or the icy river in the fields of Arretinum?
Let up, Messalla, you're too devoted to me.
Very often, my dear relation, it is not the right time for
the road.
Take me away and I leave here my mind and my feelings,
As I am subject the direction of others and not my own
decision.

Do you know that the girl's mind is relieved about the
distressing trip?
It's all right to have my birthday in Rome!
Let us all observe that birthday
Coming to you now unexpectedly.

I am not happy that you take so much on yourself on my
account
In case I am really artless and slip up.

A wall painting from Pompeii of a young Roman woman. Sulpicia might have looked similar when thinking of her beloved.

May you have a stronger desire for civil business,
Or a tart carrying her heavy work-basket
Than in Sulpicia, the daughter of Servius.
People are concerned about me and mainly worry
That I should not lose to a mattress of low status.

Do you not have a virtuous concern for your girl-friend,
  Cerinthus,
In that fever-heat now afflicts my weary body?
Ah, I would not want to overcome this grim illness

Unless I thought it to be your wish as well.
For what good would it do me to overcome the disease
If you can tolerate my sickness and not feel anything?

May I not be the intense object of your desire
As much as I seemed to be a few days ago, light of my life,
If I did not admit that I regret
Doing nothing more stupid in my young life
Than leaving you alone last night
Because I wanted to conceal my passion?

Chapter VI

PHILOSOPHICAL SELECTIONS

In antiquity, the term philosophy did not quite mean the same as it does now. At that time, their "love of wisdom" included the study of scientific as well as ethical and dialectical issues. They would investigate biology, botany, astronomy, and physics, as well as politics or ethics. The basic idea seems to have been that the world and the phenomena of the universe, including humanity, can be understood by rational analysis, and that an underlying order or system can be discerned and described.

In the Greek world there were simply a lot of philosophers of varying beliefs. As time went by, they also influenced the Romans, although on occasion under certain political circumstances they were expelled. All of these philosophers wrote many books some of which have survived. There was a somewhat different practice from that of today, since authors often wrote books of instruction in verse. We have books of poetry describing Mount Aetna, hunting game with dogs, farming, pharmacy, and other matters; philosophical subjects were not excluded. While some wrote in verse, most philosophers still wrote in prose. I begin with the former, however.

LUCRETIUS AND MANILIUS

VIEWING THE COSMOS FREES US FROM SUPERSTITION OR DEMONSTRATES THE DIVINE

I will depart from our usual practice in these pages and here include excerpts from two authors who wrote in verse, one of the

Epicurean and the other of the Stoic persuasions. Stargazing leads each to opposing philosophical conclusions. I do not intend a rigorous review of the tenets of each poet's school of philosophy. Rather, I marvel at the ability of each writer's artistic exploitation of theme in a cosmic setting. I do not mean to imply that the poetic artistry and elegance of the one is similar to or equal to that of the other. For many years Lucretius has enjoyed an elevated reputation which I believe is well justified. Manilius on the other hand is less well known and suffers from his presentation in verse of abstruse astrology, sometimes in quantitative terms. Yet his song is also compelling.

Casual use of the word Epicurean today implies having luxurious taste or habits, and the pursuit of pleasure. However, Epicurus himself was a serious philosopher, who was born on the island of Samos in 341 B.C. and lived until 270 B.C. He and his followers lived a simple life in a house with a garden in Athens. He developed a system of belief which supported an atomic theory, emphasized the physical basis of the universe and of human experience, denied divine influence in nature and human affairs, and concluded that the only rational human goal was a happy life in which pain was minimized and pleasure, when properly defined, something not to be avoided. A reasoned understanding, based on the perception of the senses, of a universe which was held to be infinite and characterized by the constant rearrangement of atoms was the ultimate basis of Epicurean moral philosophy. This system of belief held pleasure to be the goal. Value was not placed on debased physical pleasure, but on the avoidance of pain and unsatisfied desires. They asserted that contemplation and friendship eliminated competitive stress, failure, and ephemeral satisfaction. Epicurus is said to have written three hundred books, but only small pieces of his writing survive; the Roman poet Lucretius is our greatest surviving source of information about this philosophy. Lucretius, a Latin writer of the late Roman republic (his dates are estimated to be about 95 to 55 B.C.), wrote five books of dynamic epic hexameter verses, which instruct the reader in the intricacies of Epicurean doctrine with remarkable enthusiasm and art. We know little about the life of this writer, but Cicero read his long poem and tells us that he admired it. Lucretius is another author whose flickering light was preserved in only a single lamp. There appears to have been one archetype, a manuscript of the fourth or fifth century of our era which is lost, but it was copied in the ninth and tenth centuries, and we are lucky enough to have those later manuscripts.

Taking advantage of this luck, I will present a selection from early in Lucretius' work in which he praises Epicurus and tells how a reasoned study of nature and the heavens supports a superstition-free way of things, and frees us to follow a rational course in life. I have always found his enthusiasm to be appealing. I should say here that the Latin word *religio* can be translated as superstition or just plain religion. I think in his text Lucretius implies an excess of belief, and I have therefore employed the former word, but either can be used. Lucretius is a wonderful writer with all the dynamic qualities of the late Roman republic; I have included a limited extract to keep things interesting and to leave you perhaps wanting more.

When human life was lying on the earth contemptibly
Weighed down under onerous superstition,
Which was displaying its head from the zones of the heavens,
Menacing mortals from above with its terrifying appearance,
A Greek man was the first who dared to uplift his eyes in opposition
And the first who stood firm in opposition.
Neither stories about the gods, nor flashes of lightning,
Nor the menacing rumble from the sky impeded him,
But all the more provoked the keen heroism of his mind,
So that he first had the desire to break open the barriers around knowledge about nature.
Therefore the dynamic vigor of his mind was completely victorious,
And advanced far beyond the flaming battlements of the universe,
And with his intellect and will, he traversed the entire

immeasurable,
From where in triumph he brings back to us what can and cannot come to be,
And what is the basis for the limitation of force in each thing,
And its deeply inherent restriction.
Whereby superstition in turn is thrown under his feet and trampled.
His victory sets us equal with heaven.

[I omit a passage here in which Lucretius states that his position is not sinful and that on the contrary superstition is itself the cause of evil. He also touches on the nature of consciousness and the difficulty of explaining Greek philosophy in the Latin language.]

It is necessary that not sunbeams and daylight's bright shafts
But the configuration and analysis of nature disrupt the fear and darkness in our mind.
These will furnish a start for us to take on the initial idea
That nothing is ever created from nothing by gods.
To be sure, dread inhibits all mortals
Since they observe many occurrences on earth and in the heavens.
They are unable to see the reasons for these events,
And deem that they are done by divine will.
For this reason, when we shall have seen that nothing can be created from nothing,
Then we will discern more correctly that which we are aiming for,
And from what each thing can be created,
And how everything happens without divine intervention.

So there you have one rational approach to explain what we see going on around and above us. One suspects that Lucretius, as well as Epicurus, would have been very interested to learn of our biological sciences, astronomy and physics, and indeed would have felt quite at home with current knowledge and technology. However, it was, and is, possible to look at the same evidence and come to different conclusions.

The other major philosophical system I present here arising in the Hellenistic period was Stoicism. (There were other schools of philosophy in antiquity, but this chapter is not a general review.) This system was founded by Zeno beginning around 315 B.C., and takes its name from the porch or colonnade in Athens called the "Painted Stoa." It was in this location that Zeno and his followers gathered. Briefly, they believed that a divine intelligence or god guided nature and the universe, and that the proper goal of human life was virtuous behavior, which was in harmony with the laws of nature. Stoic concepts included indifference to pleasure and pain, brotherhood, the falsehood of emotion, and the self-reliance of the virtuous individual. As time went on, the school developed an elaborate system of physics, logic and ethics. Some Stoic ideas, for example, the premise that virtue is the only good and is sufficient for happiness, were attractive to the Roman psyche, and Stoicism was very popular during the Roman empire. Much of that moralizing literature has survived.

Since the Stoics believed that a divine spirit animated and harmonized the universe, it is not surprising that one of these surviving Roman authors dealt with astrology. We know nothing certain about the identity and biography of the poet Manilius, but we know from internal evidence in his writing that he composed his five books of hexameter verses during the last few years of the reign of Augustus (died A.D. 14) and the first of his successor Tiberius. He describes the stars, signs of the zodiac, constellations, the planets, comets, the methodology of the horoscope, the known world, and more in great detail. He considers all this celestial subject matter to be consistent with, and a support for, his Stoic philosophy, which he extols with great artistry in different passages through his work. I find the technical details of his astrology not as interesting as his poetic flights of philosophical argument, and also much harder to translate. I will share with you here his comments toward the end of book IV, which are as enthusiastic as those of Lucretius; I have to remind myself that he is looking at the same universe as Lucretius.

> Now nature lies concealed nowhere.
> We have surveyed all, and captured and mastered the universe.
> Integral with it, we examine our parent
> And approach the stars as his handiwork.
> Is there any question that god dwells within our breasts?
> That our spirits come from heaven and return to heaven?
> So as the universe being composed of each constituent
> Of air and lofty fire and of earth and of sea
> May direct a pervasive spirit (this line of text corrupted)
> That there are in us the constituents
> Of our earthly lot and the soul in our blood
> Which direct everything and regulate man.
> Why is it surprising if men are able to know the universe
> For the universe is in them and there is
> A small sample of god in each one?
> And is it righteous to believe that men are born
> From anywhere except the heavens?

[After discussion of the superiority of man over animals and his his use of intelligence to turn land and sea to his use and to comprehend nature and the stars, Manilius continues]

> God himself does not refuse a vision of the heavens to the globe,
> But with constant rotation discloses his countenance and physical frame
> And offers and presents himself

So that he can be well perceived and instruct those viewing
What his nature might be, and force them to heed his laws.
The universe itself calls our spirits to the stars,
And because it does not conceal, does not allow its rules to be hidden.
Who would think it a sin to know that what is righteous to observe?

I think that you get the general drift of Manilius' argument. I suspect that he was well aware of Lucretius' earlier poetic exposition of atoms and nature getting along perfectly well without any divinity as the driving force, and, to a degree, was in an artistic as well as philosophical competition. If we had all of the books of their time on these two schools of thought, the field would be much more complicated, not to say littered, with opposing argument. It is an historical accident that we have these two didactic poems of opposing philosophies in epic verse, but they do make an interesting comparison for me. The same realm of nature has a quite opposite message for our two friends from antiquity and quite probably for many of us, as well. There are fairly recent published books in which physicists explain how they see godhood in the universe, and others which take a different, contrary position. This argument actually is very current and will probably remain so.

DIOGENES LAERTIUS

DIOGENES THE CYNIC

Just as there is more than one individual named "Joe" or "Smith" today, there was more than one Diogenes in ancient times. Nothing is known about the life of Diogenes Laertius; a presumed date to the first portion of the third century A.D. is based on the lack of later dated material in his surviving work *On the Life and Thought of Famous Philosophers*. His ten books contain numerous biographical details about thinkers who are relatively well known to us currently, and many of those less familiar, in a sometimes uncritical hodgepodge of anecdotes and quotations. At times, he is of great value; for example, he is the major source for the letters, which are the main remnant of the three hundred books of Epicurus, and his description of Stoic beliefs has been well received by scholars. In many places, however, he is thought to have employed secondary sources extensively rather than the various philosophers' original writings, a practice for which he has been criticized and which probably muddles the doctrines of many of his subjects. However, I can understand the problems that he might have faced in working through thousands of papyrus rolls, if they were even all available to him, and in trying to construct a coherent presentation in an age that lacked many research tools.

He arranges the different schools of philosophy geographically and historically, and includes names we may recognize, such as Socrates, Plato, Aristotle, Pythagoras, Empedocles, Epicurus, and a number who are very interesting, but who are less well attested, and whose writings are mostly lost, such as Thales, Democritus, Aristippus, and many others. Among those whose books are gone, but whose personality has made him somewhat better known, is another Diogenes, the man known as the Cynic. This last word we use as an adjective all the time in order to describe an individual who mistrusts others' motives and the validity of traditional beliefs. Nevertheless, the word with a capital C refers to a group of ancient philosophers who shared certain beliefs about what is of value and how life should be lived. We know of this Diogenes, in part, because of his deliberately dramatic, almost ironic, posture that he assumed in order to support his position on living in accordance with basic nature. He valued poverty, physical conditioning and endurance, performed bodily functions in public, and rejected wealth, art, literature, marriage, social ranking and conventions. He lived in a large wine-barrel. To many his total lack of shame was unattractive, but his philosophical arguments must have been compelling. He may have actually invented the word "cosmopolitan". *Kosmopolites* consisted of *kosmos*, the orderly world, and *polites*, citizen, thus meaning "world-citizen".

Now the word "cynic," when applied to Diogenes, had another

A modern reconstruction of the episode during which Diogenes, living in his barrel, complained that Alexander the Great was blocking the sunlight.

implication. It is the adjective of the Greek word for dog. Diogenes held that what was natural should not be shameful, but he was attacked for behavior such as relieving himself in public, as would a dog. Now Diogenes might have felt that dogs have admirable traits; they are not fussy about personal functions, disdain clothing, recognize truths about hostility and affection, and are incapable of deception. He may have been proud of such a normally derogatory appellation. Being so known would advertise his argument that society's artificial constraints and benefits have little to do with happiness.

As you can easily imagine, such a man would become well known very quickly for his extremes of behavior, generate amusing stories, and his texts would not be likely to be copied laboriously in the very religious environments of the middle ages. Laertius does provide us with some limited and jumbled material. I have selected some of the entertaining portions, but have rearranged them so there is a little more coherence.

After he was questioned about why people make donations to beggars, but not on the other hand to philosophers, Diogenes said this: "Indeed they expect that they may become crippled or blind, but, to the contrary, not ever to practice philosophy."

When he was asked from what place he might be, Diogenes said, "I am a citizen of the world."

He went into a theater and put himself in the way of those who were going out. When he was asked about the reason, he said, "I make it a practice to do this in my entire life."

He was clever in running down others. He called Eucleides' school bad-tempered, Plato's presentation a waste of time, the Dionysiac festivals deceits for the stupid, and popular political leaders slaves of the mob. He declared that when he saw the manner of life of steersmen, physicians and philosophers, he considered man to be the most perceptive of living creatures. When, conversely, he saw dream-interpreters, their prophesies, and their followers, or those inflated with opinion and wealth, he judged none more senseless than man. He said regularly that in life either thought or a noose should be available.

He used to affirm that courage stood against chance, nature against tradition, thought against emotion.

When he was asked what was the noblest thing among men, he said "frankness".

When Plato had developed the concept that man is a two-footed, unfeathered animal, and was therefore celebrated, Diogenes brought a plucked rooster to the auditorium and said, "This is Plato's man!"

When Alexander at one time stood over him and said, "I am Alexander, the high king," Diogenes said, "And I am Diogenes, the canine."

To Alexander as he was standing over him and saying, "Do you not fear me?" Diogenes said, "Indeed, what are you? Good or evil?" When Alexander said, "Good," Diogenes said, "Who ever fears the good?"

Alexander stood over Diogenes and said to him, as he was relaxing in the sun near the gymnasium at Corinth, "Demand of me what you wish!" And Diogenes said, "Take your shadow off me!"

They say that Alexander had said if indeed he had not been born Alexander, he would wish to be born Diogenes.

He declared that nothing whatsoever in life is accomplished successfully without practice and that with it everything possible can be achieved. That in truth it is right to choose a happy life according to nature instead of pointless efforts, or being miserable because of folly. Indeed, he held as well that in continued practice the very contempt for pleasure is most pleasurable, and that just as those used to living in pleasure pass over to the opposite pleasure-free environment, so do those practicing this opposite despise the enjoyment of pleasures themselves.

Clearly, it is not possible to reconstruct Diogenes' abstract and serious argument from anecdotes such as these. Perhaps these stories give us a hint. It does seem that he liked an element of satire when presenting his position that what was natural was simple, not indecent, and would bring happiness. He seems to have thought that people were shortsighted and not discriminating in their values. His distaste for convention may be salutary or at least refreshing in our age of legalized norms, moralizing legislation and strong sense of the correct. His exaggerated simplicity, austerity and emphasis on nature would doubtless be worth pondering amid our celebrities, excessive profits and material gratifications. It would seem that he did not value the traditional material and social benefits of civilization; putting such artificial gains in their proper place may be the difficult part of his message for us. He would not replace those previous goals with other forms of self-gratification, but a more thoughtful form of self-improvement. It would not be easy to be his kind of Greek philosopher, and one would not want to end up with a form of intellectual or social anorexia. It was for this reason that "nothing in excess" was inscribed on the temple of Apollo at Delphi.

In casual terms, which were probably known to be much too simplistic in antiquity as well as now, we are told that Socrates taught Antisthenes who taught Diogenes who taught Crates who taught Zeno. The development and intellectual relations of ancient philosophy were much more complicated, but Zeno of Citium (335-263 B.C.) was the founder of Stoicism, and some Stoic concepts of austerity, independence, and living in accordance with nature may sound familiar to an admirer of Diogenes the Cynic. Stoicism itself evolved after Zeno and was an elaborate, sophisticated and ethical system by the time of our next author.

MARCUS AURELIUS

THE HUMAN SPIRIT

It is surprising how many ideas from antiquity remain familiar in our sensational, electronic, ephemeral age. Many school and college graduates are familiar with the idea of the philosopher king. Some may remember that it was an idea of Plato and have actually read his idealized *Republic*, in which a special class of ruler was specially educated. A benign idea, perhaps, if carried out with the original beneficial intention but perhaps cast in a bad light by the evil absolutists and dictators of the twentieth century. Many will say that it was a good idea, although that it has never happened and can never happen, but in my opinion they are incorrect. It has indeed happened in the history of the West. Once. In A.D. 161. In March of that year Marcus Annius Verus was installed by vote of the senate of Rome as *princeps*; he is known to us as the emperor Marcus Aurelius. It appears that he had always been a very studious and sincere boy, attracted from an early age to the rigors as well as the pleasures of serious philosophy. He impressed the emperor Hadrian who called him *verissimus* meaning that he never pretended to be somebody that he was not and was intensely honest. He was educated in depth by the best teachers available, and a good selection of his letters to one of his instructors, Fronto, survives. In these letters we see that already at a young age Aurelius is serious and to be respected.

Aurelius seems to have been an unusually moral ruler, devoted to duty and virtue. In one of history's tragedies, a man so interested in human well-being was faced with extremely serious foreign invasions in the East and in the North, as well as a deadly plague. At times barbarian tribes even invaded Greece and Italy. There was a revolt in the East as well. Therefore, this man of philosophical good will spent many years under canvas while he commanded the Roman armies in the field. When he was not so engaged, he was heavily involved in the affairs of state. As a Stoic, he viewed such duty as becoming and right and proper for a man.

Besides what is revealed in the letters of Cicero, no other ancient, and perhaps modern, historical figure's inmost thoughts are as open to us as those of Marcus Aurelius. Through circumstances that are not well understood, we now possess twelve books of his personal musings, which are currently, named *Meditations* but which the manuscripts indicate are "to himself". These were not intended for publication, but clearly, after his death, someone saved them and we are the richer for that act. He dwells on reason, nature, acceptance, and virtuous acts from an almost transcendental perspective. He wrote in Greek, not Latin. That may have been his practice because his extensive education in philosophy depended on the study of Greek books, but I also suspect that he found increased personal satisfaction in putting his ideas in order in a language different from what he used for everyday business. If I may compare a pebble with a pyramid, I often found Latin literature a support or solace after a day in the operating room dealing with malignancy.

With such a rich and thoughtful source, it is difficult to select one reading over another. Although Aurelius followed Stoic teaching, there is material from other systems, and he quotes Epicurus favorably. I would say in passing that we should remember that this work was not written by an academic or a professional philosopher, safe in a library or study, but by the master of the Roman world, the commander in chief of the legions, on whose day to day orders and overall strategic concept the safety of the threatened nation depended. His was the bloody sword and the implementation of law. I imagine him after a day's rigors, in his tent at night musing and composing these mighty thoughts. Stoicism is not a philosophy for sissies. It requires structured mental concentration and I think is a harsh, but rewarding, mistress. It is I believe one of those endeavors that offers the greater gain for the greater effort. What some commentators have called pessimism in the work I would consider rather as clinical realism. The task of the philosopher is to rise above the limitations of time and ability that mortals face. Some have even called Stoicism therapeutic. At times in life, rational and calm acceptance of the inevitable is desirable, and I have seen many such situations.

> The duration of the life of man is a speck, his essence dissipating, perception by the senses indistinct, the composition of the whole body prone to rot, the mind a whirling motion, fortune unpredictable, and fame is doubtful. To speak briefly, on the one hand everything of the body is running water, on the other everything of the spirit is dream and mist. Life is a battle and the transient visit of a stranger. Fame is forgetfulness. What then

The bronze equestrian statue of Marcus Aurelius. The emperor is depicted as very thoughtful, even soulful.

is capable of conveying us through? In this only philosophy. This to protect the spirit within as to be not ill treated and unharmed, master over pleasures and pains, neither acting rashly, nor altogether falsely and hypocritically, not dependent on what someone else does or does not do, moreover accepting what comes along and what

> is allotted, as coming from that place from where, from whatever source, it came itself. Beyond everything, awaiting death with gracious opinion, as only another setting free of the elements from which each living being is compounded. However, if it is not terrible for the elements themselves that each is continuously changed into something different, why might anyone have misgivings about the change and disintegration of all things?

The patience and perspective of this passage have always moved me. There is a deep humility here, but also an awesome strength that allows Aurelius, and, we hope, in imitation ourselves, to move along the path of virtue and good works despite the reverberation of Acheron. Yes, one can look up at the flaming battlements of the universe and see duty.

Chapter VII

MAGIC, GHOSTS, MONSTERS

Recent successful films employ recurring themes; among them in the horror genre are stories about evil practitioners with magical powers who can change into a bat or a wolf, or about tormented spirits that wreak havoc on wretched mortals. You have probably already surmised that I am going to show you that these are far from new concepts, but may be very thankful that this chapter looks less serious than the one previous.

It is my guess that novel reading, at least in terms of coarse numbers, generates much, if not most, of publishing activity today. A look at the selections in this book and the titles of the great majority of surviving ancient texts might lead one to believe that the literary consumer of antiquity had markedly different tastes from those of readers of today. We should remember that the constituents of what has been preserved are due to the forces of history and the preferences of scholars of subsequent ages. There were many novels in ancient times and actually a number have survived intact. We have in complete form five Greek novels written mostly during the time of the Roman Empire. They contain love stories; typically a couple deeply and truly in love are separated, endure many dangers such as pirates, shipwrecks, powerful rivals, false deaths, and then are happily reunited at the end. Sometimes the action takes place in what was, for the time they were penned, a historical setting.

APULEIUS

THE WITCH IN LOVE

With the exception of very late Latin translations of some Greek originals, for the Roman novel we have only one complete example, the *Metamorphosis* by one Apuleius of Medaurus, a town in the Roman province formed from what had earlier been Masinissa's Numidia. Apuleius was probably born around A.D 125 .; he was well educated, and had an interest in Platonic philosophy. We have some of his autobiographical and rhetorical writings, but he is best known for his long novel.

Magical or divine transformations of humans or gods into different shapes were a common and popular theme of mythology and popular belief, and ran a wide gamut from the story about Zeus, the king of the gods, placing himself in the form of a shower of gold pieces into the lap of a woman to whom he was attracted, to out and out witchcraft. In Apuleius' novel, a somewhat satirical quality is added to metamorphosis since Lucius, the hero of the piece, is turned into a donkey or ass. (Film also seems to have rediscovered the idea of an intelligent donkey.) In that form, still self-aware but unable to speak, he endures a variety of dangerous, sometimes erotic, sometimes farcical, adventures. A tapestry of related stories is interwoven into Apuleius' ample eleven books; there are descriptions of organized crime and profit-seeking cults, but perhaps best known and most attractive of the attached tales narrates the romance of Cupid and Pysche, in which the god of uncontrolled passion and sudden desire is himself affected by emotion and ardor, and there are, as is usual in ancient love stories, ordeals to be endured before the happy ending.

In northern Greece, the territory of Thessaly had a reputation as the haunt of powerful and pitiless witches, who could perform many awesome feats of magic. Apuleius, through the daring of the main character Lucius and his friend Fotis, details the magical technique of one Pamphile in whose home he is staying as a guest-friend of her husband. First, Pamphile tried to lure in her intended lover with a potion compounded of, among other gruesome things, pieces of buried people. When this attempt failed, the witch decided to change herself and fly to her favorite instead. Lucius and his beloved kept themselves busy in amorous adventures while they were waiting.

> After a few nights were passed in this kind of sensual pleasure, Fotis, excited and very exhilarated, ran up to me, and disclosed that her lady-mistress, beause she had not yet made any progress in her amorous intentions, on the very next night was going to feather herself and turn into a bird, and in that guise fly down to the man she wanted. I was therefore to observe a thing such as that with caution. Then early in the night, Fotis herself, with deliberate and silent steps, led me to the witch's elevated chamber, and told me to observe what transpired through a certain crack in the entryway. The first thing Pamphile did was to take off all her clothes, and then she opened a small strongbox and took out quite a few cosmetic jars. She took the cover off of one of them and took some ointment from it. She rubbed it between her hands for a long time and then applied it all over herself from her toes to the top of her hair. She spoke much that we could not hear to her oil lamp, and waved and wiggled her quivering limbs, on which as they shook small soft feathers erupted, and strong wings grew. Her nose curved and became hard, and her nails were formed into a hooked shape. Pamphile became an owl! In that shape she emitted a complaining cry, then, testing the way little by little, she sprang off the ground, and finally, carried high aloft, flew out and away with her wings spread wide.

The witch could assume any shape she wished, and fly away to work her will. There may be a slight element of satire in this metamorphosis into an owl, the bird sacred to Athena. A nightingale or a sparrow might have been more appropriate to a love-tryst. The choice of an owl may indicate that Pamphile, no matter how steeped in magical skills still does not quite get it. We find it entertaining that the lover Lucius is turned into a donkey, and that a lovesick witch changes into an owl, but some transformations are not so benignly amusing.

PETRONIUS

THE LYCANTHROPE

Petronius, writing under Nero, tells about a different transformation. He wrote a novel in at least sixteen books, of which we have only one book and some other fragments. It was at least in part a work of satire and described rather unfavorably the social life of freed slaves, and demonstrated vulgar or spoken, as opposed to literary, Latin. The story of Petronius himself did not end happily, as he was compelled to commit suicide when out of favor with the emperor in A.D. 66. Nero forced a number of other suicides by literary and political figures at that time. In the following passage, the tasteless host at a dinner party has trotted out a freedman acquaintance, who it appears is valued for his story which the other guests prod him to recount. He does not need much encouragement. Here is the tale that he recounts at the dinner table.

> At the time when I was as yet in servitude, we were dwelling in a narrow alley. Now the house is Gavilla's. It was there that, just as the gods wished, I began to fall in love with the wife of Terentius the innkeeper. You knew Melissa the Tarentine, a very pretty little piece. By Hercules, I was not troubling myself about her for physical reasons or on account of lust; but rather because she was good-natured. If I needed anything from her, it was never refused to me. She made a copper coin; I had half. Whatever I had I entrusted to her safekeeping; I was never deceived. Her mate met his last day at the country house. And so I strove by hook or by crook for a way to have a relationship with her. However, you know friends

A painted Greek vase depicting a man under the skin of a wolf. About 450 B.C. There were traditional Greek and Roman mythologies and religious festivals which were connected with the wolf. Ceremonies on Mount Lycaeus in the Arcadia region of Greece were thought to cause metamorphosis into the shape of a wolf.

show themselves at critical times. As it happened, my master had gone off to Capua to arrange some appropriate minor business. Taking advantage of the opportunity, I convinced a friend of mine to come five miles up the road with me. And indeed he was a soldier, strong as Pluto himself. We went off in the evening, the moon was shining as though it were noon. We came up to some tombs; my friend began to be busy near the monuments. I sat down to rest and count the memorials. Then when I looked back at my companion, he unclothed himself and placed all of his garments close along the road. I held my breath and stood as if dead. But he urinated around his clothing and suddenly became a wolf. Do not think that I am joking; I would accept no inheritance, no matter how great, to lie about this. But, as I had begun to say, after he became a wolf, he began to howl and ran away into the woods. At first, I didn't know where I was, then I went over to pick up his clothes, but they had become stone. Who was there to die of fright except me? But I drew my sword and I struck at shadows for the whole way until I reached the country house of my lady-friend. I went in like a ghost, my spirit almost blown away, sweat rolled off me in two streams, my eyes were dim, I was barely resuscitated. My Melissa was surprised that I was walking out so late, and then she said, "If you had come before now, at least you might have assisted us, since a wolf came into the estate, attacked all the animals, and bled them like a butcher. But he did take note of us, even if he ran away, since our slave pierced his neck with a spear." After I heard that, I could not keep my eyes shut any more, and when it was light, I fled to the house of my Gaius as though I were an inn-keeper that had been robbed. After I came to the place where the clothes had been made into stone, I found nothing except blood. In truth when I got home, my soldier was lying in his bed just like an ox, and a physician was treating his neck. I knew that he was a were-wolf, and thereafter I could not break bread with him, not if you killed me. Some may

> consider what they may think about this matter; if I am a liar, may I have all your guardian spirits angry at me.

This sort of story is not unfamiliar; we can say the same about the next selection.

PLINY THE YOUNGER

THE HAUNTED HOUSE

We have already met the younger Pliny in a previous chapter. Here is another of his letters, which describes a report that he had heard. Pliny's story is not about shape-changing and is presented with his usual polish.

> A house at Athens was spacious and roomy, but in disrepute and unhealthy. In night time's quiet, you heard the clank of iron, and if you paid close attention, the rattle of chains, at first at a distance and then close by. Then an apparition used to appear, an old man, weak, gaunt and dirty, with his beard grown out and his hair standing on end. He wore shackles on his legs and chains on his hands and he was shaking them. Because of him the occupants of the house were in fear, stayed awake, and spent grim and fearful nights. Their sleeplessness was followed by sickness and death amid growing terror, since, although the specter was gone, during the day also the memory of the ghost drifted before their eyes, and the terror persisted longer than the cause of it. Therefore, the house was abandoned, remained vacant, and was entirely left to the specter. Nevertheless, it was advertised in case anyone who would wish to purchase it or to rent it might be uninformed about such a major curse.
>
> Athenodorus, the philosopher, arrived at Athens, read the advertisement, and, taking note of the low price, did

a thorough investigation, and, rather than being discouraged, was all the more ready to rent. When evening began, he ordered things to be laid out for him near the entry of the house. He asked for notebooks, a stylus and a light, and he sent all the rest of his people deeper inside the building. He himself focused his mind, eyes and hand on writing, lest his unoccupied mind should invent phantom sounds and insubstantial terrors on its own. At the beginning, there was night time quiet as there would be anywhere. Then occurred the sound of iron being struck and rattling chains. Athenodorus did not raise his eyes, or release his stylus, but stiffened his resolve regardless of what he was hearing. Then the noise increased, it came closer, and was heard at first as though at the door, then inside the door. He looked behind him, saw and recognized the phantom that had been described to him. It was standing there and was motioning with its finger as though calling him. For his part, Athenodorus signaled with his hand that the ghost should wait a little, and again he applied himself to his stylus and wax tablets. The ghost made a great noise with its chains right over his head as he was writing. When he looked back again, the ghost was making the same signs. Athenodorus did not delay, picked up his lantern and followed. The ghost proceeded with a slow pace as though weighed down by its chains. After it turned into the yard of the house, it suddenly disappeared and left Athenodorus by himself. He, now alone, marked the spot by pulling up leaves and plants. On the next day he advised the town officials that they should have the place dug up. They found bones that had been shackled and entwined in chains, and the body, having decomposed with time in the ground, had left the bones naked and eaten away by the fetters. The bones were gathered up and buried at government

> expense. Thereafter the house was free of the properly buried spirit.
>
> And I believe the above since there are those who assert it to be true.

In this letter, which I have not quoted in its entirety, Pliny recounts two other tales and appears to ask the addressee what he thinks about ghosts and whether they exist or not. He writes this query to Licinius Sura, a very important contemporary political figure, a consul and a close associate of the emperor Trajan. Pliny implies that he is judging the possible truth of the matter very seriously.

All of the above stories, whether related in works of fiction or in a letter of inquiry, do tell us what kind of folk-tales and fantasies were prevalent in ancient times and how little changed they are from today's written and film productions. This similarity probably tells us something about our taste for this genre, which may be, I am afraid to say, a trans-generational interest.

Chapter VIII

PHILOSOPHY THEN AND PSYCHIATRY NOW

There were similar kinds of jobs in antiquity and now. Both ages have had many soldiers, farmers, sailors, architects, politicians, writers, merchants, bankers, surgeons, explorers, athletes, and boxers. There is a long list of parallel professions. However, as I have commented previously, there does seem be a notable difference. Most towns and urban areas in antiquity were tenanted by philosophers, sometimes quite numerous, if not contentious. They belonged to different schools of thought, but they provided a variety of educational and intellectual services. There is no city in America today without a number of offices in which psychiatrists and psychologists practice their skills and provide services to their communities. Certainly in antiquity there was awareness of mental illness and the Roman writer Celsus describes some very gentle and humane methods of management for such patients. However, more recent creative medical skill was able to take famous Greek and Latin stories and devise a symbolic analysis of the nature of certain human defects and, in so doing, to affect profoundly our concept of individual and social human nature. I am not here venturing an opinion on the validity of the psychoanalytic theory of mental development and pathology created by a clearly brilliant thinker in a sexually repressed, patriarchal society. I encountered patients' personality disorders, neuroses and psychoses in my practice of urology, and had to deal with delusions and paranoia that affected clinical management. I am quite sure that such problems occurred in antiquity. I would like show two selections and try to demonstrate how our ancestors thought about these stories in a manner quite different from what have become our cultural clichés. Describing such differences may be much easier than determining what is valid, and discovering any significant lesson concerning how we think about ourselves.

SOPHOCLES

OEDIPUS THOUGHT HE KNEW WHAT HE WAS DOING

The Athenian dramatic poet Sophocles was born in 496 B.C. into a successful and liberal family, and lived to an advanced age. During his lifetime, Athens experienced the establishment of democracy, victory over the threat of Persian tyranny, and a rich artistic flowering, but in his later years there was the Peloponnesian War which was a dreadful struggle with Sparta. In addition to writing plays, Sophocles served the public in both civilian and military official appointments. At that time the dramas of the Greek playwrights were not just for entertainment, but were vetted productions of serious cultural import presented at major public festivals, and officials judged them for possible honors and awards. The employment of comments by a chorus, as well as stories or subject matter familiar to the audience, allowed this author to concentrate on studied nuance of the human experience rather than the unraveling of a plot. In some ways, the situation might have been comparable to our annual viewing of a nativity play or a version of Charles Dickens' *Christmas Carol* during the holiday season in December.

Aristotle thought that Sophocles' best work was his *Oedipus the King* which was a product of the poet's mature years. Now lost are a much earlier poem about Oedipus which was part of the epic cycle, as well as a play by Aeschylus, and Sophocles' play, which has survived, is our definitive version of the story. Most are familiar with the outlines. Oedipus as a baby is the subject of an oracle that predicts that he will kill his father and marry his mother. His parents, in order to avoid such a result, pierced his feet and sent him out to die; kindhearted individuals save him and he is brought up elsewhere. When, as an adult, he becomes aware of the dire prediction, he leaves what he

The young and heroic Oedipus confronts the sphinx.

thinks is his home city and kills an unknown man, actually his true father, on the road to Thebes where he then slays a monster called the Sphinx. As a reward, Oedipus is given the kingship and the queen, his actual mother, as his wife. The action of the play concerns Oedipus trying to do the right thing and discover who murdered the previous king. To the eyes of Oedipus, everything that he has done, being a good king after slaying the Sphinx, has seemed proper, right and just. He is devastated when he learns the truth about what he has done in actuality and after he rushes off stage the chorus comments:

> O generations of mortals!
> So we do appraise your lives as valueless,
> For what man achieves the fullness of joy,

Or seeming to do well, then descends?
Holding your example before me, O sad Oedipus,
And your sad fortune, we call no mortal happy.
Aiming high you prevailed in every success,
And, O Zeus, destroyed the maiden monster Sphinx
Who had crooked talons and spoke a verse riddle.
You rose up as a tower of defense for our land from her murders
From which you are called our king,
And gained the highest honor, being the lord ruling in great Thebes.
Who now do we hear to be more wretched?
Who, afflicted by life-change in savage ruin and distress?
O the renowned eminence of Oedipus!

Ah Oedipus! He rids Thebes of a murderous monster and ends up in bed with his mother. A dangerous and honorable deed leads him to the violation of sacred prohibition. Sophocles employs the dramatic metaphor that it is only after he is blind that Oedipus really sees what he has done and the truth of the situation. In antiquity, he was a metaphor himself for the human condition. A man whose feet have been crippled walks the path of life with difficulty to a destined fall. Thus Sophocles teaches that the results of our best-intentioned actions can be very negative indeed. Oedipus clearly did not want to kill his father and make children with his mother, and thought that he had been doing something very different as a good and highly valued king of Thebes. Man has limited understanding, and may be circumscribed by truth taking the form of an immutable and universal destiny.

In our current cultural context, the story of Oedipus symbolizes desire for the mother and aggression against the father at an early stage of "infantile sexuality." Sometimes, in order to explain mental pathology, these issues are thought not to have been resolved properly by adulthood, or the concept may be used casually and socially to explain everyday issues with relationships. In this theory, our human identity is composed of deep-seated conflicts and desires. These may be inconsistent but are considered to be mutable and treatable.

We have here two very different concepts. In one, the human condition is defined by circumstances and limited abilities characteristic of our nature. In the other of today, our nature is held to be in inner conflict, but perfectible. These two differing views of human nature based on the same story are important for the interpretation and implementation of law, social policy, and even art. Before we explore these issues further, let us look at how another story from mythology is used to depict a personality disorder.

OVID

THE EXCESS OF NARCISSUS

We have already met the poet Ovid in a previous chapter. Although there are a few other fragments, his is the definitive source for the story of Narcissus, and it may be that he put his own artistic stamp on the tale. Before we go on with this text, I will remind you that the expression "nothing in excess" was engraved on the temple of Apollo at Delphi. This concept, that it was not proper and even an anathema to the gods to go beyond the bounds of reasonable human behavior, was basic in antiquity. Those who were arrogant and immoderate were expected to be subject to retribution, sometimes thought to be the work of the goddess Nemesis. Our ancestors looked for her to provide a punishment that would, sometimes quite artistically, fit the crime. In Greek morality, there was the concept of retribution. This definition of hubris appears, according to some scholars, to have been willful or deliberate insulting behavior to another, what we would call today disrespect. Balance in behavior would be an ancient version of the "norm".

To continue with our poet, we have seen his art in the verse form known as the love elegy. As noted previously, he also wrote other works: poems about heroines of mythology, a scholarly calendar, but possibly of greatest interest to us is his fourteen book work *Metamorphoses* which, despite some textual difficulties, has survived intact. Ovid was steeped in ancient literary tradition and provides us with much wonderful material, but tinctured with his own personal vision. His retelling of the popular story of Narcissus was famous in antiquity as well as in modern times. The beautiful but unfeeling and arrogant Narcissus is visited with an exquisitely appropriate retribution. Here is Ovid's version. This passage is the longest of my selections, but I could not decide what part to leave out.

Narcissus turned sixteen and looked like a boy and a young man at the same time.
He was an object of desire for many young men and women.
But there was such hard disdain in his soft physique
That no youth or girl ever even touched him.
A nymph who had a certain gift of speech caught sight of him
As he was chasing into a net some deer that he had started.
It was Echo, who repeats,
Who knows not how to be silent when someone is speaking,
And not to speak first herself.
At that time Echo still had a body and was not yet just a voice,
But she was still loquacious, and had the same mode of speech as now,
That is, she repeats the end of a series of words.
Juno did this to her because when she often could have caught
The mountain nymphs in the act with her husband Jupiter,
Echo was clever enough to delay the goddess in long conversation
Until the nymphs could escape.
When Juno learned what was happening

She warned Echo about decreased use of her false tongue
And an abbreviated voice.
And the threat came true.
Echo still repeats the last words of a statement
And mimics each one that she hears.
And so when she saw Narcissus roaming the back country
She took fire
And followed his trail in secret
And the more she followed him
The more she glowed with a brighter flame.
Just like quick sulfur is smeared around the top of a torch
And ignites as a flame is brought near.
How often she longed to approach him with blandishments and sweet-talk.
Her natural disposition held her back and didn't permit her to initiate anything,
But did allow her to be ready and waiting for sound
That she could send back as though her own words.
It chanced that the boy was separated from his loyal band of companions,
And called out, "Is anyone here?"
And Echo answered, "Here!"
He was surprised and looked sharply all around.
Then in a loud voice he called out, "Come here!"
She said what he said.
He looked around again and when nobody appeared said,
"Why are you staying away from me?"
And he heard back again exactly what he had just spoken.
He stood in one spot and was tricked by the semblance of another's voice.
Then he said, "Let us join together!"

And Echo, never more eager to reply to any sound that she has ever heard,
Replied, "Let us join together!"
She herself followed up what she had said and came out of the woods
To throw her arms around his neck that she desired so much.
He broke away and as he ran off said,
"Get your clinging hands off me!
I would die before I could be involved with you!"
She answered only, "I could be involved with you!"
Rebuffed, she kept out of sight in the woods,
And hid her humiliation among the leaves,
And from then on lived in secluded caves.
But still her love persisted and grew with the pain of her rejection.
Despair kept her awake and attenuated her woebegone form.
Emaciation puckered her skin and all the fluid of her body evaporated into the air.
Only voice and bones were left.
The voice remains; they say her bones were turned to stone.
From then on, she has hidden in the woods,
And is no longer seen on any mountain ridge.
All can hear her; just sound lives on in her.
In this way, Narcissus amused himself with her,
With other water or mountain nymphs, and with companies of men
Before finally one of the rejected raised hands to the sky, and said,
"Just in this way may he himself fall in love;
Just in this way may he not possess his beloved!"
Goddess Nemesis who has her temple at Athens

approved his just prayer.
There was a clear pool of spring water
With a silvery shiny surface,
Touched by no shepherd or nanny-goat browsing on the mountain-side,
Or any herd animal.
No bird or wild animal or branch falling from a tree
Ever disturbed it.
There was grass around the edge, which the adjacent water supported
And woods which kept the sun from warming the place.
Here Narcissus, tired out from the heat and the exertion of hunting
Lay down after he had seen the surroundings and the spring.
And when he wanted to decrease his thirst,
Another thirst grew,
And as he drank, he was captured by the appearance of the figure that he saw.
He loved an incorporeal hope and thought a shadow to be a true form.
He was astounded by himself, kept the same expression; he did not move,
And remained fixed to the spot like a statue shaped from Parian marble.
Settled on the ground, he gazed at a double star, his bright eyes,
Hair fit for the god Bacchus, fit for the god Apollo,
Young cheeks, a neck of ivory,
The beauty of his countenance,
The pink flush in combination with snowy, luminous white.
He wondered at everything for which he himself was wonderful.

All unaware, he wanted himself,
He who cherished was himself cherished,
Was pursued while he pursued,
And ignited and burned at the same time.
How often did he set useless kisses on the deceptive pool?
How often did he dip his arms to reach for the neck that he saw in mid-water
And did not lay hold of himself in it?
He knew not what he saw, but what he saw burned him.
The same mistake deceived his eyes and stimulated them.
O beguiled boy! Why pursue fleeting images in vain?
What you want does not exist!
If you draw back, you lose what you love!
What you see is the shadow of a reflected image!
It has nothing intrinsic to itself.
It comes with you, it remains with you;
It will leave with you—if you can leave.
No desire for bread or respite could drag him away from there,
But, lying spread out on the shady grass,
He scrutinized the false image without any satisfaction,
And perished through his own eyes.
Lifting himself up a little, he held out his arms to the surrounding forest and said,
"Has love ever treated anyone more cruelly?
You know the answer since so many have used you as a suitable hideaway.
Since your life encompasses so many ages of time,
In your long existence do you remember anyone who withered away like this?
He is delightful and I see him, but what I see and is delightful

One of the paintings from Pompeii of Narcissus at his pool. Echo rejected and pining is on the left while on the right Narcissus attended by little Eros is fixated on his own reflection.

I still do not find.
Such uncertainty has fastened upon my ardor,
I am unhappy all the more since we are not kept apart
  by a great sea
Or by a mountain, or by closed gates in a wall!
We are hindered by a scant amount of water!
He wants me to hold him!
As often as I offer a kiss to the clear water
He comes up with his lips below me!
You would think it was possible to touch him.

What stands in the way of our love is the least little thing!
Whoever you are, come out here!
Why are you tricking me, oh incomparable boy?
Where do you go when I come after you?
For sure it is not my looks or my age that you are evading.
Why the nymphs also love me!
You offer some kind of hope to me with your friendly face,
And when I extend my arms to you, on the other side you extend yours!
When I laugh, you laugh back,
I have often observed your tears when I am weeping.
You return my motion with your own nod.
And as much as I can guess from the movement of your beautiful mouth
You return words that do not reach my ears.
I can feel it!
My likeness did not deceive me!
I am burned with self-love.
I both generate and carry the flame!
What should I do?
Should I coax, or be coaxed?
What I desire is with me.
My own riches make me needy.
O, would that I might be able to separate from my body!
A new prayer for a lover: I would wish that which I love should go away from me!
Already misery carries away my vitality and I have a short time left to live,
And I die at an early age.
Death is not a burden for me; it will put away my misery.

I would wish that he who is the object of my affection would live longer;
Now we two as a single spirit will perish in harmony."
After he spoke he was barely rational and went back to looking at the same visage,
And roiled the water with his tears.
An indistinct image was reflected by the rippling pool.
He saw it going away and called out,
"Where are you running to? Stay here! Don't be heartless!
Don't abandon me while I am loving you!
Let me at least look at what I can't touch and gratify my sad passion!
While he despaired, he pulled down his shirt
And struck hard at his naked chest with his marble-colored hands.
Under the blows his chest acquired a rosy flush
As does fruit when it is shiny-white in one part and ruddy in another;
Or as different clusters of grapes that are not quite ripe
Assume a crimson shade;
He also saw this effect in the water that had again become clear;
He could not endure any more,
But as yellow wax commonly melts in light heat,
And morning frost in the warmth of the sun,
So he, weakened by love, dissolved,
And little by little was diminished by hidden fire.
And then his complexion was no longer white with a tincture of rose.
And neither his energy nor his strength nor his charm remain,
Nor did the form of his body, which Echo loved.
Although still provoked and unable to forget,

She still felt sorry when she saw him,
And as often as the pathetic boy said, "Ah woe!"
She reproduced the words, "Ah woe!"
And when he struck himself, she also reproduced the same noise of breast-beating.
With his customary look into the water,
These were his last words.
"Ah boy, uselessly adored!"
And the place gave back just the same words,
And after he said "Farewell", Echo said "Farewell" too.
He lowered his exhausted head onto the green grass.
Death closed the eyes that were still cherishing the image of their owner.
And after he had been admitted to the underworld,
He kept watching himself in the waters of the Styx.
His sisters, the water-nymphs, mourned him,
And cut their hair for their brother.
The wood-nymphs mourned.
Echo repeated the lamentations.
And then they were making ready his bier and funeral pyre,
And waving the funeral torches.
His body was nowhere.
Instead of his body, they found a flower with white petals
Surrounding yellow in the middle.

Well, there you have it: one guilty of excess caught like a fly in honey. In his own honey in this case. Ovid is dealing with illusion, the limits of human understanding and the need for social balance without extreme individual behavior. Destiny or the gods provide a framework within which the human story is told. Ovid dramatically elaborated a well-known and popular story, and demonstrated considerable metrical skill when he depicted echoes in his verse. His story clearly is one of dreadful divine punishment, and I would guess that many of us might feel a sense of relief after finishing the tale of Narcissus, and be pleased that we have not gotten ourselves into such a situation by some kind of inappropriate behavior.

The Fourth Edition of the *Diagnostic and Statistical Manual of Mental Disorders* describes the Narcissistic Personality Disorder as being characterized by grandiosity, a sense of entitlement, lack of empathy, and other traits that most of us would consider unattractive. There is a variety of personality disorders such as antisocial, obsessive-compulsive, paranoid, up to the total of ten. There are also authors who have a broader view and use the term "narcissism" with more general and less strictly clinical implications. Yes, there is self-absorption, but Ovid has drawn for us a picture of misery and delusion. Ovid's Narcissus is trapped in a deadly punishment, which is a reflection of his own excess. That Ovid would have thought of Narcissus' problem as social need not deter us from our own era's interpretation of the story in psychological terms. A personality disorder, after all, represents a persistent and pervasive abnormality of thought and behavior patterns that markedly affects an individual's role in society. We were taught in medical school that a little bit of suspicion, a little bit of self-importance, a little bit of wanting to be alone are appropriate and make up a normal personality, but that when one such component becomes the exclusive foundation for thought and interaction—well then you have a problem. When our instructor made that point, all of us in the classroom looked at each other and laughed nervously.

Where does that leave us with Oedipus and Narcissus? Their stories do provide convenient shorthand for complex ideas in psychiatry. Nevertheless, I do believe that when we look at the original texts there is something to learn that is equally profound. You have read the whole of Ovid's story of Narcissus. You may wish to read, or reread, the whole play of Sophocles about Oedipus the king. Then you can decide for yourself what may be the message of these tales from our ancestors. They were written at a time when there were many, many philosophers. These stories may be multi-layered enough to offer both philosophy and psychiatry. On the one hand, will we accept that there is inevitability to human life and that as we go along, although we pretend otherwise, there is a necessary future that we cannot sense? Alternatively, can we treat ourselves, change our course and our destiny? Much of our current law and social policy and political discourse implies that we believe the latter. No matter what Oedipus does, no matter what Narcissus does, they follow a course that is not clear to them, but is well evident to the reader. You will have to decide what that discrepancy means, and yet . . . and yet, mythology and art might just be reflections of philosophy and psychiatry.

Chapter IX

WATER SACRED AND POTABLE

There is a science of water and there is a religion of water; its purity, sources and use have been important since the times of first recorded history and probably earlier. Clear water, drinkable and safe and issuing up from the surface of the soil, might have a scientifically understood ground water source or it might be considered to depend for its cleanliness and sweet taste on a spirit whose power keeps it intact and renews it. Many Americans when casually opening a tap, may not give much thought to the source and processing of their drinking water. Our bodily metabolic processes require enough water intake to produce about a liter of urine a day; the amount varies depending on age, habitus, weather, and physical activity. Generals, businessmen, kings, premiers, clergy, and many others have all exploited water's scarcity or plenitude. Water, especially potable water, has always been in short supply and may be expected to be a source of regional conflicts in the years ahead. There have even already been disagreements between the states of Georgia and Alabama about sources of fresh water. The role of water in contemporary religion is very familiar. Most Christian denominations employ water in the initiation ritual of baptism which word is derived from a Greek word *baptizein* meaning to wash or dip. Water which is blessed by a Catholic priest and used in certain ceremonies is called "holy water". For Hindus there are seven sacred rivers and the waters of the Ganges are especially purifying. There are special vessels to hold water and many rituals employing water. For Muslims water provides two types of purifying ablutions. There was extensive ritual washing with water in historical Judaism and some of this practice remains. In Japan waterfalls may be sacred. The reader may very well be familiar with other issues of faith involving water.

The importance of water in earliest antiquity led to civilizations settling alongside the river Nile in Egypt and between the Tigris and Euphrates rivers in Mesopotamia – that is the land between the rivers. Greek and Latin writers were fascinated by the Nile and its fertilizing not to say life-giving annual inundations and there was much speculation about the causes of the rise and fall of this great river.

PAUSANIAS, OVID AND SERVIUS

ARETHUSA AND ALPHEUS

Among the needs that we share with our ancient ancestors is the necessity for a plentiful or at least adequate supply of water that is palatable and free of toxins or disease causing organisms. In Greece and Italy as well the clear water of springs was favored. Many springs were sacred and possessed an attendant deity, usually a water nymph. A variety of divine or healing powers were associated with springs, and it is easy to see how a steady source of safe water might have been thought to be provided and protected by a female divinity. Many springs were quite famous and the subject of noble writing. One of the most well know was the sacred spring of Arethusa.

When colonists from the Greek city of Corinth founded Syracuse in 733 B.C. on the east coast of of Sicily, they first settled on the adjacent small island of Ortygia. In part this site may have been selected because of the clear water of the Arethusa spring which is still present today. Syracuse became the foremost Greek city of antiquity, but never forgot the divine presence at her origin. About three hundred years after the city's founding, its mint depicted Arethusa when it produced the most famous and beautiful coin of antiquity and perhaps of all time, the great ten drachma piece by the artist Euainetos.

There are different versions of the charming myth which explained Arethusa's presence in Sicily. About A.D. 150 an author named Pausanias, who was a Greek from the west coast of Asia Minor, wrote

The great ten drachma coin created by the artist Euainetos for the mint of the Sicilian city of Syracuse. The portrait depicts Arethusa herself surrounded by dolphins.

Description of Greece in which he described in ten books virtually all of the great traditional points of interest—monuments, religious sites, topography—of Greece proper. He often added interesting associated tales. In chapter seven of book V he comments briefly on the relationship between the river Alpheus in the Pelopenesse region of southern Greece and the Arethusa spring in Sicily.

> Thus it is said in regard to Alpheus, that he was a huntsman, and had a passion for Arethusa, and that she also hunted. They say that Arethusa, unprepared for mar-

riage, crossed over to the island opposite Syracuse, named Ortygia, and there from human became a spring, and that for Alpheus, also under the influence of love, a change into a river came to pass. This entire tale in regard to Alpheus <?and to Ortygia> (*The text here is corrupt. Lines describing Alpheus making his way from Greece under the Ionian Sea to the island of Ortygia on the coast of Sicily were possibly skipped by the copyist and lost.*) It cannot be that I will doubt that passing through the sea there he mingled his water with that of the spring, knowing as I do that the god in Delphi spoke confirmatory words, and that when he sent off Archias of Corinth for the colonization of Syracuse also said and composed the following:

A certain Ortygia lies in the dark sea,
Across from Trinacria where the mouth of the
Alpheus gushes forth
And streams to mingle with fair-flowing Arethusa.

We now turn again to the Roman poet Ovid, quoted in two previous chapters, whose literary ability presented a somewhat different and more dramatic version, which I cannot omit when we are considering what we may characterize as the free flow of divine waters. The passage is from book V of his *Metamorphoses* which he probably finished about the time of his exile from Rome in A.D. 7. His Arethusa, was a nymph in the train of the divine huntress Diana. Although beautiful, she was modest and shy of male attention. Hot and tired after hunting in the woods, she came upon an inviting stream which she did not know harbored a river god named Alpheus. The goddess Ceres is asking her a question.

"Why did you run away, Arethusa?
Why should you be a sacred spring?"
The waters become still as the deity lifts her head from

the deep spring.
She wrings out her green hair with her hand,
And recounts the old time love of the Elean river.
"I was one of the nymphs who are in Achaea,
And no other worked her way through through the woodlands more enthusiastically,
And no other set out the hunting nets more enthusiastically,
But although I never wanted to be well known for my beauty
And although I was strong, I had a reputation for beauty,
And I was not pleased with the excessive praise for my appearance
In which others used to take great delight.
I was embarrassed by my body's bucolic endowments
And thought it a sin to be desirable.
I was tired, I remember, and I was returning in the Stymphalian wood.
It was hot and exercise had doubled the heat.
I found waters without a strong current, flowing silently,
Transparent all the way to the bottom
And through which each stone was easily counted,
And which you would hardly think to be in motion.
A grove of white willows and a poplar nourished by the water
Were shading the sloping banks with their native growth.
I drew near and at first dipped in the sole of my foot,
Then up to my knee.
Not satisfied with that, I undressed
And placed my light clothing on a bent willow.

Nude I sank into the water.
While I was smiting the water and splashing,
As I was slipping along in a thousand positions,
As I paddled with my arms,
I noticed I knew not what undertone below in the midst of the flood,
And terrified I ran up on the edge of the nearest shore.
'Where are you hurrying to, Arethusa?' Alpheus called from his waters.
'Where are you hurrying to?' again he spoke out to me in his coarse voice.
Just as I was without my clothes I ran.
My clothes were on the other bank.
All the more he pursued me and all the more he was amorous.
And because I was nude I seemed to be more ready for him.
In this way I was running, in this way he was chasing me fiercely.
Just as doves fly away from a falcon with agitated wings,
Just as the falcon usually presses after the agitated doves,"

Ovid describes Arethusa running through a large number of Greek towns with obscure names, and then continues.

"I maintained my speed and he was not faster than I.
But I was not his equal in endurance and could not endure a long race,
But he could tolerate an extended effort.
Still I ran on through fields, through mountains veiled in forest,
Rocks as well, and cliffs, and where there was no track at all.

The sun was at my back.
I saw a long shadow going out before my feet,
Unless it was a vision of fear.
Yet for sure the sound of his footfalls was frightening,
And his forceful exhalations puffed on my hair-band.
Worn out by my effort to escape, I called out,
'Help your weapon-bearer, oh Diana,
Whom you often have had carry your bow and quiver of arrows!'
The goddess was moved and brought down
One of the thick clouds and threw it over me.
Alpheus searched all about me while I was concealed in mist,
And all unknowing looked for me around the hollow cloud.
Twice he circled around the location where the goddess had hidden me,
And twice he called for me: 'Ho! Arethusa! Ho! Arethusa!'
What were my grim thoughts then?
Like a lamb that hears the wolves howling outside the barn?
Like a rabbit lying hidden in a thorn bush
That perceives the hostile faces of dogs
And does not dare to move its body at all?
And he still did not leave
For he could not find any of my footprints that receded.
He kept watching over my cloud and my location.
A cold sweat took over my afflicted limbs
And blue-green drops trickled down from my entire body.
A pool gushed out wherever I set my foot,
And moisture fell from my hair.
More quickly than I can recount the story for you now

I was changed into the fluidity of a spring.
But the river Alpheus recognized my water that he loved
And, setting aside the the man's appearance that he had assumed,
He changed into his very own waters
So that he might blend himself with me.
Diana of Delos split open the soil
And I, submerged in concealed caverns, was transported to Ortygia
Which I cherish since it is named for my goddess
Who first brought me up to the air above."

The river Alpheus, the modern Alfeios, drains the southern territory of Greece (the Peloponnese), and empties to the West into the Ionian Sea. The fresh water of the modern Arethuse spring still flows at Syracuse in today's Sicily. In antiquity, perhaps in part because of cultural connections between that part of Greece and Syracuse, it was believed that there was a connection under the sea between the Greek river and the Sicilian spring, and that the water of the former flowed into and mingled with that of the spring. This delightful notion is attested in many ancient writers.

Interest in such an imagined connection between the Sicilian spring and the Greek river probably developed soon after the foundation of the city of Syracuse and definitely persisted until late antiquity. *Scholia* is a term that refers to ancient notes on Greek or Latin writers. Many of these have survived and we have fairly complete a late fourth century A.D. commentary on Vergil's poetry by one Servius. He comments on the story of Arethusa and Alpheus in a related passage in Vergil.

According to story she was a huntress who while she was washing herself in Alpheus after her labors became the object of his passionate love. When Alpheus perceived that she was hiding in the form of a bird, he pursued her

> even so changed. After she had been running from him for a long time, she was changed by the pity of the gods into a spring named after her and came to Sicily through secret passages. Alpheus followed her all the way there and mixed himself in with her spring. And here is the proof: when the horses that compete during the Olympic holidays are washed off in the Alpheus river, the horses' dung from that river is also identified in Arethusa. Also a wine bowl which a certain Olympic victor had dropped into the Alpheus river is said to have been found in Arethusa. Vergil also showed that she was a huntress when he said that swift Arethusa had laid aside her arrows. But some believe that Arethusa did not come from Elis to Sicily but was born in Sicily and met the river when he arrived.

One would quickly be aware if the water supply had developed a foul odor, and many of the calls to water departments today complain about smell or taste. Today we would explain an unpleasant scent in a spring's water by contamination of the ground water by methane or volcanic sulfur. A little later in this chapter we will review the sources of modern municipal water supplies.

Many springs in ancient Greece and Italy were endowed with beneficial female spirits. Greek water nymphs were called Naiads. One of the most famous springs in ancient Greece was Hippocrene, on the slope of Mount Helicon and sacred to the Muses. It was thought to have been started when the winged horse Pegasus stamped his hoof. Outside the Capena gate in Rome there was a grove of trees containing a spring inhabited by the Camenae, water spirits friendly to the Vestal Virgins and later considered to be Roman muses. Divine attributes for sources of safe drinking water were not just a peculiarity of antiquity. In the British Isles most holy wells have been renamed for Christian saints, but often their associated pagan practices have been preserved. Such wells or springs were thought to be sacred long before the advent of Christianity. Miraculous healing or fertility powers are still attributed to such waters now. In Scotland a "clootie well" may have a nearby tree on which a rag or cloth dipped in the spring water is tied. Such a "clootie" accompanied by a prayer to the associated saint or spirit will carry away an illness with it. Sometimes one must walk around the well or throw in a coin. These activities may represent early Celtic ceremonies. Interestingly there is a town in Cambridge-shire actually named Holywell where an annual ceremony of well dressing, a form of decoration, was revived in the 1920s. Here we may also note the report of the Roman scholar Varro, who wrote about the Latin language around 47 to 45 B.C., and described the annual Roman fountain festival, the *Fontinalia*, when on October 13 the wells were also decorated. Pliny the Younger (A.D. 61-112) whom we also met in an earlier chapter wrote an elegant letter in which he described the source of the river Clitumnus which had an olden temple and statue of the local deity as memorials to other spirits. The location and the stream that it fed were a place of scenic beauty.

VITRUVIUS AND FRONTINUS

PUBLIC WATER SUPLIES

SAFETY AND DISEASE

Beyond mythology there was a practical point for our ancestors as well as us – the need for a stable supply of drinking water. Some towns and even cities in antiquity were founded near a spring, but more highly engineered solutions were required when urban populations increased. Ancient Rome by the beginning of our era is thought to have had a population of over a million. Clearly one or two simple wells or springs would not be adequate. The Romans, with their propensity for civil engineering, studied the qualities of water supplies and how to make them available to urban populations. Under Augustus Caesar there was an extensive public building program and we have a complete set of ten books dedicated to him by one Vitruvius, an architect of the time. He appears to have lived and worked during the mid and latter part of the first century B.C. It appears that early in his career he managed the artillery of Julius Caesar's army and that later he provided architectural services for the emperor Augustus. Vitruvius discusses a variety of subjects: architectural theory, building materials, temples of different style, public buildings, theaters, theory of harmony in music, public baths, harbors, homes, clocks, machinery, military devices. Much of Vitruvius' work summarizes previous Greek theory and demonstrates a detailed and broad knowledge of famous lost Greek authorities, although his Latinity is not cultivated or literary but technical and possibly closer to the every day spoken language. Nevertheless his work continued to be read and influenced the development of later European architecture. What will interest us here is his discussion of potable water supplies and their qualities. He was well aware of the importance of a good and safe water supply for the public well being.

> Therefore springs that are beneficial for human life must be sought and selected with the greatest care and effort. Tests and inspections of such springs should be seen to in this way. If they will be free flowing and lying open, before starting to draw water off, let the men who live near these springs be studied and analyzed to see what limb formation they may have. And if they shall have strong bodies, fine skin, flawless limbs, clear eyes, then the water will be very acceptable. Likewise if a new spring has been made by digging and its water, when used to wet a vessel of Corinthian brass, silver and gold amalgam or of another type from good bronze, has not left a stain, will be of the best quality. And likewise if that water is boiled thoroughly in copper and then left still and poured out and no sand or muck is found in the copper bottom, that water also will be approved. Likewise if peas or beans are put together in a vessel with

> that water and placed over the fire, and are quickly completely cooked, they will demonstrate that the water is good and healthful. None the less if the very water which is in the spring is clear and transparent, and moss or rush does not grow where the water reaches or flows out, and the location is not polluted by any filth but has a clean appearance, these indications assure that the water is pure and of the greatest healthfulness.

Once you have a plentiful and salubrious supply of water, it has to be distributed, and indeed Vitruvius has a chapter on aqueducts and piping. He discusses the technical details of the construction of piping, describes a descent of at least one half foot for every hundred feet for adequate gravity feed, reinforcement at points where the pipe changes direction, and provision for the release of air trapped under pressure. I find of very great interest Vitruvius' comments on the best material to use for water pipes.

> Nevertheless distribution by ceramic pipes has these advantages. First if any defect has been made in the work, whoever you please is able to restore it. Also water from such pipes is much more healthful from clay pipes than from lead pipes because through lead it seems therefore faulty since white-lead comes from it. This latter substance is said to be injurious to the human body. For if something hurtful is produced from a substance, there is no doubt that the substance itself may also not be healthful. For we can note the example of workers in lead because their bodies demonstrate sallow hues. For when lead is poured out to be cast the vapor, pervading and then searing the organs of the body, extracts the potency of the blood from their limbs. Therefore it appears that water should be distributed as little as possible in lead pipes if we want to have it hygienic.

In the United States lead piping was installed until well into the twentieth century. Of course now the health implications are well known and the use of lead for potable water supplies is restricted. Even now however there are a few lead pipes here and there. Lead pipes in homes in the United States were not used after about 1930 but lead containing solder for copper pipe connections might have been used until 1986. It appears that areas where soft water is present are more at risk for human injury than areas where the water is hard. Lead pipes were used for many years in New York, Massachusetts, England and Scotland and there were many adverse health effects. Officials were slow to replace lead pipes, possibly due to the cost.

Lead is readily absorbed after oral intake, especially by children. It can also be inhaled and I did have such a patient in my own practice who had been stripping lead paint in an expensive part of town. Lead is carried by the blood throughout the body, crosses the blood-brain barrier and is stored in the skeleton. Lead interferes with cellular metabolism, especially the activity of mitochondria and can cause abdominal pain and lethargy in children and can affect intellectual development. Adults experience abdominal, head and joint pain, irritability, muscle weakness, and forgetfulness. There can also be kidney damage. Accurate blood tests to establish lead levels are available and are diagnostic. Everyone in medical school is taught about the "lead-line" at the border of the gingiva and the teeth, but this is uncommon and seen after long heavy exposure to lead. In any case it looks as though Vitruvius was correct.

The only relatively "pure water" is distilled water. Natural water always contains dissolved minerals and gases. For example calcium in ground water can vary from 1 mg to over 4000 mg per liter. There are similar but smaller variations for magnesium, sodium, potassium, bicarbonate, sulfate, and chloride. The pH, the acidity and alkalinity, also vary. Because ground water is always in contact with rocks and minerals, and moves more slowly than surface water, ground water usually has more dissolved mineral content than surface water. Solution is enhanced because ground water tends to be warm and acidic. Much ground water has a total level of dissolved solids of less than 250 mg per liter but the figure can be much higher. For comparison sea water contains about 35,000 mg per liter. When water contains a good amount of dissolved solids it is termed "hard". High calcium or magnesium are common offenders. When calcium reacts with the sodium stearate in soap an insoluble precipitate is formed. These calcium or magnesium salts form the scum that one sees when trying to lather up in hard water. In general soft water has 0 to 60 mg of solids per liter and hard water over 120 mg per liter. The FDA classifies mineral water as coming from a natural underground source and containing 250 parts per million of total dissolved solids. The various combinations of these dissolved minerals give these waters their often distinctive and very pleasant tastes. There are also sometimes claims of health benefits from drinking, or bathing in, various mineral waters. Some bottled water companies have been accused of adding mineral compounds to tap water. I noticed this activity myself when reading the label on one popular brand. Added trace minerals may include magnesium sulfate, potassium chloride, or sodium chloride.

There are a variety of types of mineral springs: sulfur springs with hydrogen sulfide gas, alkaline springs, radioactive springs, hot springs, springs containing iron salts, and others as well. In the United States there are towns named Sulfur Springs in Indiana, Oklahoma, West Virginia, Montana, Colorado, and Texas. Some towns are just called Mineral Springs. And in the United States there may be a commercial aspect to mineral springs which are often associated with motels or resorts. There are health claims for bathing in such waters. So called balneotherapy is thought to treat arthritis, fibromyalgia, chronic pain, stress, muscle aches and other ills. Europeans are familiar with the idea of the spa. The only hot springs in England are found in the area of Bath, and the waters were probably an indigenous holy site before the Roman conquest. The Romans built temples at the site then called *Aquae Sulis* and associated with the goddess Minerva. After the Norman conquest a bishop was in charge, and in Georgian times the town was a major spa and health resort. In Germany Baden Baden was known to the Romans as a site for baths and was known as *Aurelia Aquensis*. In these and many other facilities in North America and Europe health benefits were and are often touted from

The water supply open to the public at the side of the road in North Stonington, Connecticut. Water flows continuously from the exposed pipe. Note the disclaimer.

drinking the water or submersing in it.

Somehow springs provide traditions of myth and magic for us. The line between understanding the safety and technical qualities of water and just faith in the excellence of a given spring even today may be very finely drawn. There is a natural water source well known to the local population on Route 9 in North Stonington, Connecticut.

For some time it had been used by those who thought highly of its potable and natural qualities. In the past the town government determined to close off the facility since it was being used freely and the water was not processed or tested to be safe for human consumption. So much public protest ensued that a compromise was reached. The water pipe would be left at the side of the road and freely available, but a sign was posted which warned that the water was not authorized for human use. Of course the end of the pipe through which the spring drains is near the road and one can see containers being filled there by the public very often.

Augustus' architect, Vitruvius, has told us about pipes, but it is an author of a little later period that has provided a detailed description of the famous system of aqueducts that provided a bountiful supply of fresh water to ancient Rome. Sextus Julius Frontinus was probably born around A.D. 35, and had a military career in which he was selected as consul and suppressed revolts in Gaul and Britain. In A.D. 97 he was appointed by the Roman emperor Nerva to be in charge of the system of aqueducts. We are left with two of Frontinus' works, four books on military affairs and two books on the aqueducts of Rome. The latter give us priceless documentation about the Roman water supply and its management, and, equally significant, insight into the mind of an upper level Roman administrator. I find his attitude towards an extremely technical subject quite enlightening. Remember that he was a political appointee.

> Since every commission from the emperor requires very close attention, and since either my natural conscientiousness or diligent fidelity stimulate me not only to industry but also to love for the commission, and since now the directorship of the aqueducts, affecting the needs, moreover the health and also the safety of the city, has been laid on me by Nerva Augustus – I don't know whether he is an emperor more hard working for, or more affectionate of, the state—and always managed by the leading men of our city, I judge it primary and most

> important, as has been my practice in other business, to know about what I have undertaken. And I am confident that there is no more certain foundation for any business. Or any other way to discern what is to be done and what is to be avoided. Or nothing so unseemly for a respectable man as to conduct a commission according to the instructions of subordinates.

I am sure that you have an opinion about how well our own contemporary political appointees learn the details of their administrative responsibilities, but the main point here is that public water supplies should have knowledgeable and hard working executive officers. Frontinus goes on and describes in sequence the construction history of the nine aqueducts which supplied the city of Rome, their dimensions, the water sources, details of their design, their output of water, and the laws which governed their administration. He goes into great detail and the casual reader of his two books might found the recounting of pipe calibers and water flow daunting. Some commentators have observed that more water per person flowed into ancient Rome than in many modern cities. In the midst of this professional recounting Frontinus exhibits some Roman pride in an off hand remark.

> Compare, as is easily seen, the inactive pyramids, or the other idle but renowned works of the Greeks, with the many essential weighty structures for so many waters

One of the reasons that so much water was supplied to ancient Rome may have been the popularity of large public baths. Reconstructions of these structures show impressive buildings, even by today's standards. There are many ruins or remnants of Roman baths, some huge and public and others included in private residences that may be seen in Bath, England, in Rome and elsewhere throughout the Mediterranean world. The daily bath is not just an American invention, but much socializing as well as bathing was done in Roman times at such facilities.

At this point in our discussion we may ask the question what happens if the water supply is not safe or sanitary. There is a famous example from more recent history. During the year 1854 in the Soho district of London there was an epidemic of cholera that ultimately resulted in over six hundred deaths including many children. Cholera is an infectious disease of the intestinal tract caused by a rod-shaped motile bacterium called *vibrio cholerae.* In 1883 the great Robert Koch visited Egypt, discovered this organism and how it was transmitted in drinking water. (Beginning in 1876 he earlier had described the bacterium that causes anthrax and then demonstrated that microorganisms were the cause of infectious disease thus solving an age-old mystery.) Cholera causes a devastating diarrhea which does not cause severe cramps but produces huge volumes of gray liquid stool. It rapidly depletes the fluid and electrolytes of the body. These rapid and heavy losses, which today can be readily treated either by intravenous or properly constituted oral fluid replacement, result in volume depletion, dehydration, shock, kidney failure, and death. If water and salts are replaced mortality is extremely low.

In 1849 an English physician, John Snow, published an early work which presented an accurate theory that cholera was water-borne and contracted orally. At that date he did not know the exact cause of the disease but won a prestigious French prize. During the London epidemic in 1854 he created a map of the affected area which showed the cases clustered around the public water supply pump on Broad Street (now Broadwich Street). Dr. Snow told the local authorities that if the handle of the pump were removed that the epidemic would ease. And that is what happened. Later investigation showed that the pump's water was contaminated by human waste. The removal of the handle of the Broad Street pump is a famous initial event in the history of modern epidemiology and public health. A sad footnote is that later the local authorities were not convinced and replaced the handle. The episode reminds me a little of the decision in North Stonington to leave the unprocessed spring water available with only the protection of its accompanying signage.

A variety of illnesses is water-borne. Viral diseases such as rotavirus, which affects young children, and Norwalk virus, which can also affect adults, can be spread by drinking water contaminated by human waste as can hepatitis A. There are other bacterial illnesses which can be spread by the oral route. One of my physician friends has described to me his bout with typhoid when he was young in the Indian sub-continent. Fecal contamination or breakdown in disinfection processes could allow the bacterium that causes typhoid, *salmonella typhosa*, to be distributed in the water supply. Although we almost never think of typhoid in contemporary American or European society, we should remember that in the fairly recent past that the disease was widespread and the cause of death of such notables as prince Albert, the husband of queen Victoria, and Wilbur Wright. Current sanitation techniques and processing of potable water supplies have made typhoid extremely rare in North America. Protozoan intestinal infections comprise another category. Amebic dysentery in the United States is not commonly water-borne, but two other protozoans have attracted considerable attention. *Giardia Lamblia* is a common parasite of American wildlife, is resistant to the usual techniques of disinfection of drinking water and has caused a large number of human cases. I recall another medical colleague who was very ill with this infestation and lost twenty pounds.

In the spring of 1993 an epidemic of abdominal cramps and watery diarrhea affected the residents of Milwaukee, Wisconsin. The illness lasted one to two weeks and affected about 430,00 people. At least 54 deaths were attributable to the epidemic. Study demonstrated that the causative organism was *cryptosporidium parvum*, a protozoan parasite taken in orally in the form of cysts that originate in human or animal solid waste. This event in Milwaukee was the largest outbreak of water-borne disease ever reported in the United States and the total expense was thought to be around one hundred million dollars. Epidemics caused by disease carried by drinking water are rare in the United States but a recent article in the literature reported that between 1971 and 2002 there were 764 reported outbreaks with 57,557 cases of illness and 79 deaths. These events are for the most part thought to be due to incomplete or interrupted municipal water treatment. Most often an organism such as cryptosporidia is found in surface water rather than ground water and is removed by filtration rather than disinfection.

There are two main sources for community water supplies: surface water and ground water. Larger communities or cities require large sources such as rivers, lakes or reservoirs which fall into the former category. Water supplies of this type are exposed and susceptible to chemical or biological contamination. Ground waters, ultimately replaced by rain, are found in subterranean aquifers and are sometimes under pressure. These sources are accessed by natural springs or by wells, and generally are of a higher sanitary quality due to underground filtration processes and less exposure to casual contamination as may be the case with surface waters. There have been problems however, such as admixture of toxic chemicals from landfills. Current standards for safe drinking water establish maximum levels of organic and inorganic compounds such as lead or lindane. A special class of reaction products may form when organic substances in surface water supplies are exposed to traditional chlorination. A well known study in 1987 showed a higher risk of bladder cancer in those who drank chlorinated surface tap water for over forty years in comparison with who drank unchlorinated ground water. However there are naturally occurring contaminants as well. Radium 226 can be added to ground water as it makes its way underground. Radon, a short-lived noble gas, is continuously produced by the radioactive decay of the radium 226 present in rocks and soil. There is even evidence for its generation from the surface of the moon. Radon is a carcinogen, acting through the products of its own radioactive decay, and acts as a cause of lung cancer by inhalation rather than ingestion. Radium 226 has a half life of only 3.8 days and is itself a product of the decay of uranium 238 which is widely distributed in the earth and has a half life of 4 and a half billion years. Thus the supply of radon will never be exhausted, at least in our lifetimes.

Although there is much government regulation directed towards the control of toxic substances in drinking water, the threat of illness from viruses, bacteria and protozoans remains. Despite these potential problems most of us, myself included, open the faucet, fill a glass and drink calmly without a thought of where the water has been and what has been done to it. Usually such confidence is justified. There are several methods of treatment for municipal water supplies. Sometimes when the water is acidic the pH is adjusted towards the basic or alkaline. The process called flocculation clears particles out of the water by coagulation into larger sized particles that are then initially removed by sedimentation in holding areas. A sand filter may then be used for the next step of filtration. Lastly disinfection is carried out by adding chemicals that oxidize and kill pathogenic bacteria. Chlorination has been the traditional method, but there are other commercially available techniques such as producing a hypochlorite based disinfection with electricity in a brine solution, which has worked well in my community. The per capita use of water that has been processed by municipalities in the United States is probably between 150 and 200 gallons a day. On average we only drink a gallon or less a day, but we use our precious potable water to wet the lawn, wash the car or the floor, and perform a host of other activities. Yet bottled water is at least a thousand times more expensive than what comes out of your tap at home. Every day the thousands of municipal water plants carry on their never ending efforts to provide safe drinking water. The personnel do not seem to get the appreciation that they deserve, no medals or speeches, but I am sure that if there were ever a problem they would get lots of attention. Without drama or honor they save lives every day. But, as some times happens, if you ever receive an order to boil your water before drinking it, be sure and do it.

HORACE

THE BANDUSIAN SPRING

In the midst of all these technical considerations about urban water supplies, we sometimes may forget the charm and beautiful esthetic associated with wells and springs. The cool waters, associated greenery, and natural grace can make a moving and wonderful impression. There are many descriptions in ancient literature of such beautiful sites, but the famous ode of the poet Horace to a spring near his birthplace comes readily to mind.

O spring of Bandusia! Clearer than glass!
Worthy of sweet wine and flowers!

. . . .

You as well will become one of the illustrious springs,
As I tell of the oak set over the rocky cavity
From which your murmuring waters cascade down.

Chapter X

TRANSMISSION

Human persistence and, at times, luck have provided us with remarkable and relevant messages from our ancestors. Our parents' parents' parents and so on. An average of two thousand years separates us from the Mediterranean sunshine that illuminated their days. Perhaps about seventy or eighty generations have passed and I do not think that anyone has a family tree going back quite that far. It is nowhere near enough time for significant evolutionary change such as the kind that separates us from the Neanderthals or Homo Erectus; biologically the Greeks and the Romans are the same as we. Yet there is a cultural difference, an historical separation, you will say. You might also say that I have shown you lots of piquant passages, but they are from a long time ago. I will argue that it is just that distance, just that historical gap, which endows what our ancestors had to say with so much perspective and realism.

The preceding thirty-nine selections only exist for our benefit because a series of individuals saved them, as well as all the rest of what we have. To simplify, the preservation of our Latin texts was accomplished by careful copying at the great medieval monasteries such as Cluny, Bobbio or Monte Cassino. There had been a revival of learning under Charlemagne, which even generated a highly legible form of script, and as well as ensured the reproduction of what were at the time already centuries-old manuscripts. Many Greek texts were collected and saved by Byzantine scholars, such as Photius and Arethas, and then later circulated in the West during the early

Renaissance. If one excludes political or religious motives, there are probably two kinds of reasons why you or anyone else would save or copy a book. Either there is admiration for the subject matter and the style, or the book itself is treasured as something fine. For me, at least, there seems to be a special pleasure when lines of peerless poetry or prose are seen on patrician pages.

There may be a sensual pleasure to the physicality of a book itself, which leads to a heightened sense of what is to be cherished and might not be just ephemeral. In ancient, medieval and modern times, there have been books remarkable for the clarity of their letters, quality of papyrus, vellum or paper, art and decoration, and skill in construction or binding. Over the centuries these books have been a pleasure to hold and admire, as well as to read, and in some way reflected the grace of the author. In our day of machine made paperback, not to say electronic readers, produced for a mass market, the book as a work of art is not an obvious concept. Clearly it is a good thing that Aeschylus is available in inexpensive paperbacks for so many more readers than he could have reached in a limited number of laboriously hand-written rolls. As a result his surviving work will never be lost, but there are still many who appreciate the nuances of fine paper and bindings.

CICERO

BOOKS ARE WONDERFUL

Less materially, there is the certain attraction of what has been written. I sometimes imagine a monk in the Middle Ages, perhaps a little drowsy in his corner of his monastery's scriptorium, reading with wonder and anticipation words penned a thousand years before, and describing events or thoughts of a lost golden time in the sun of ancient Italy or Greece. The digression about books by Cicero during his defense of the poet Archias reads as well to us as it did to our monk, but for us it may ignite the glow of universality rather than awe. In the following passage, Cicero has just provided us with a list of famous Romans of his history, men who were renowned, but still characterized by self-discipline and learning derived from books. Cicero continues:

> . . .who to be sure, if they were not helped by their education in defining and enhancing their abilities, would never have devoted themselves to study. But even if such a benefit were not anticipated, and even if pleasure were the sole reward of these disciplines, still my opinion is that you would judge this mental exercise to be most humane and enlightened. Other pursuits are not suitable for every time, age or place. These studies nourish youth, delight old age, add luster to success, provide a refuge and consolation for misfortune, please us at home, never interfere with business, stay up at night with us, travel with us, ramble in the countryside with us.

Then, as now, thoughtful observers valued their books for their instructive, if not ennobling, examples and admirable precepts. Certainly many volumes were sophisticated, salutary and absorbing, although the elder Pliny did remark that there is no book that is so bad that there is not some good in it. In a more serious vein, Cicero does note elsewhere in his speech for Archias that talent, rather than learning, most often induces success, but that the combination of both results in the finest outcome. Some in antiquity, especially the author of the next selection, were indeed concerned with what composed a lofty style, and the propensity of humans to select out and appreciate the best.

LONGINUS

ON THE SUBLIME

The true identity of the author of the work titled *Peri Hupsous*, or *On the Sublime* as it is traditionally translated, is to a degree a mystery.

The names attached to the ninth century A.D. manuscript, "Dionysius or Longinus," are not really consistent with any well-known ancient writer and may be in error. Likewise, there are differing opinions about the actual date of composition of this work, which in more recent times has been important in the history of literary criticism and theory. Current opinion tends towards a date in the first century B.C. More significant is the loss of scattered pages amounting to perhaps a third of the original text.

Our author discusses literature of a lofty or elevated nature at length, identifies different stylistic techniques, and gives demonstrative examples from authors of the highest reputation such as Homer and Demosthenes. Our so-called Longinus demonstrates much discretion and taste and in the following passage he writes movingly and passionately about the implications of great writing for the human condition. In doing so, he may provide some insight into why so much effort was expended under sometimes difficult conditions to preserve the ancient texts that we do possess.

> . . . and this precept in addition to many others: that nature selected man not to be a base and inferior living creature, but, as if having brought him into a vast concourse, into life, and into the entire cosmos, made him a spectator of her games and a spirited contestant. Right away she inflated our spirits with an irresistible desire for everything great, and more divine than ourselves. Indeed, the whole of ordered creation is insufficient for the grasp of human contemplation and understanding, but yet our thoughts pass beyond the boundaries of the firmament around us. If one looks around at the circle of life and how much in all things the extraordinary, the great, and the beautiful take precedence, for what we were created will quickly be seen. Thus, it is natural for us to admire not the little streams even though limpid and useful, but the Nile and the Danube and the Rhine, and even more the Ocean. And we are not impressed by

Fires in the sky. The Pleiades. The constellation of the seven daughters of Atlas, sisters among Tennyson's "silver braid."

> the little flame that we light,even if it stays bright, more than by the lights in the heavens . . .

Longinus is arguing that the finest essence of being human is to pass beyond the animal attractions of our material appetite and to seek out our destiny in the illumination of abstract thought, artistic endeavor, and new insights and understanding. Such a desire, I believe, inspired our ancestors during dark times to preserve ancient literature in which thoughts shone out like stars.

I have tried to provide some of the promised color with which I have painted my leisure time. This final selection I hope provides a little more perspective as well about the passage of this color through time and space to us.

SENECA THE YOUNGER

THE NEW WORLD WILL BE FOUND

You have probably surmised that, if there was a Seneca the Elder, there would be a Younger as well, and you are right. The second son of the elder, he was born in Spain and brought to Rome at a young age. He studied grammar and rhetoric with the leading educators of the day and after a period of political exile in Corsica was appointed as tutor by Agrippina, second wife of the emperor Claudius, to her son Nero, who was twelve years old at the time. Seneca followed Stoic teachings and much of his writing about the moral aspects of that philosophy has survived. He also had a public career, was a senator and became the senior adviser to Nero as emperor. His influence diminished with time as Nero became more tyrannical, and he was forced to commit suicide in A.D. 65 Some hostile current opinion accuses him of hypocrisy and non-Stoic behavior, but he acquitted himself well when ordered to kill himself, and I think that a degree of compromise in pursuit of at least some public good is not unreasonable. Working with Nero must have required some flexibility.

Seneca is known to have written about geography, but the work is lost. His *Natural Questions* do survive, although in disordered form. He had a long-term fascination with the subject that he finally did write about when he was probably around seventy years old. He reviewed meteors, rainbows, thunder and lightning, large rivers, wind, and earthquakes. At the beginning of his book on earthquakes, he mentions the quake of A.D.62, which occurred in Pompeii before the famous eruption of Vesuvius in A.D. 79.

Seneca also wrote nine dramas, which we have, and I am going to show you a short selection from his play "Medea," which I will think will be of interest to those of us who live in the Western Hemisphere. The foreign princess Medea had been brought home by Jason in the Argo, the first ship, and the chorus has been talking about the changes that the boldness of sailors had achieved and the opening up of the sea as a highway to distant shores.

> Now already the deep sea has yielded
> And submitted to every wish.
> The renowned Argo, constructed by the hand of Athena,
> And carrying the oars of kings, is not required.
> Any skiff wanders all around the deep.
> Every boundary has been removed,
> And cities place their walls in new lands.
> The earth is easily passable
> And leaves nothing in the place where it had been.
> The man from India drinks the cool river Aras in
>   Armenia,
> The Persians drink the Elbe and the Rhine.
> An age will come in future time
> When Ocean will release the bonds of its expanse,
> And a great land will stand open,
> And Tethys, Ocean's wife, will reveal new worlds,
> And Thule will not be the farthest of the lands.

Thule is not the modern Thule, but was six days' sail beyond Britain and may have been Norway or Iceland. It was the classic expression for as far away as you could go.

Well, the above was written in the early sixties A.D., about fourteen hundred years before Columbus. "Ocean" was, in mythology, the god of the deep water that was thought to circle the known world, but with the development of more rational geography the name came to be associated more with the watery vastness beyond the Pillars of Hercules. As I mentioned previously when I introduced Lucian's trip to the moon, the ancients knew that the earth was a sphere, and Eratosthenes, in the latter part of the third century B.C., calculated the circumference of the earth with surprising accuracy. (For your interest, Hipparchus in the second half of the second century B.C. calculated the distance to the moon accurately, as well.) I can only speculate here, but it is not unlikely that someone thought that land was necessary on the other side of the sphere of the earth to balance the known world. Seneca may have read something that made him add this comment in a mythological drama.

Is it possible that there was some rumor about the Americas? There have been much speculation and popular literature about early, undocumented contacts between older civilizations and the Western hemisphere. One recent popular book argued that Chinese sailors reached the East and West coasts of North America in A.D. 1421, a thesis that has not been generally accepted. The most intriguing data point with which I am familiar is a small terra-cotta head that was found in 1933 in a pre-Columbian burial in Mexico and which appears to be consistent with second century A.D. Roman style. Was it a hoax or a real find? I don't know, but if real, it certainly raises some interesting questions. I have a friend whom I respect very much who about thirty years ago sailed a twenty-foot sailboat, with one other crew, from Gibraltar to the Caribbean Sea. There were many trading peoples in antiquity who were very capable sailors indeed, just as capable as my friend. I think that they would have had the technical capability to follow the prevailing winds in the South Atlantic Ocean to the West Indies. I am not sure if they could have found their way back, and I am certainly not sure if they ever did it. Apparently, there is good archaeological evidence that the Romans were in the Canary Islands. From there who knows?

Still, there is one thing that we do know. The Greeks and the Romans have come to the New World in books. Their theories, their history, their observations, and their advice are all freely available to us any day of the week. We do not have to sail to a strange location or unearth a forgotten site. All we have to do is turn a page.

AFTERWORD

I have had this project in mind for many years, but it is only since leaving active medical practice that I have had the time for completion. When I revisit authors who were the object of my youthful admiration and learn now about some whom I have not known previously, I find that I sometimes find new answers and sometimes new questions. Consequently my gratitude for those who guided my education at Brown and Nichols School, Harvard College and Boston University School of Medicine never decreases. As I have progressed through life, my admiration for the men to whom this work is dedicated has only increased.

I am surprised that as I have gotten older my enthusiasm for the material in this book has also increased. I suppose this appreciation is what has directed me towards trying to share what I have enjoyed with you the reader. I fear that I am showing off my collection of precious purple passages, and my friends with whom I discuss these writings often say that they must be terribly difficult to understand. For these reasons, I have tried to show that these ancient discourses can be pertinent to the present day. I will be very glad to receive your comments by email at ancient.purple@yahoo.com, and will try to answer if possible.

I wish to thank my publisher, Britt Bell, for his thoughtful help with this project. He is experienced and wise. I also thank my wife Mary; her skilled correction of grammar, punctuation and style has been invaluable. She is most knowledgeable but above all patient with me. Geoff Goodman has added refinement and clarification. Christine Kong has reminded me of my delight when I first read classical texts, and that they offer fresh insights to young and old students. Many, many thanks as well to professor and author Robert Leuci for his invaluable advice and encouragement.

The responsibility for error is mine alone.

Μοῦσαι γὰρ ὅσους ἴδον ὄθματι παῖδας
μὴ λοξῷ, πολιοὺς οὐκ ἀπέθεντο φίλους.

CITATIONS

If you really do want to see more of any of the authors who wrote the selections in the previous pages, I list the citations in order of appearance below. There are numerous editions of some of these authors. Many appear on the internet and are available at no cost, but one must beware of stilted or very formal translations, especially in older works. The use of archaic English may be especially inappropriate when translating language that was originally quite lucid. In addition, there are other superb writers from ancient times whom I have not quoted in these pages such as Homer, Tacitus, Aeschylus. Horace — the list is very long. There are guides to the surviving ancient literature, both in book form and on the internet. If you have a strong interest in a specific area, for example love stories or architecture, you will be able to find something to interest you. Here are the references to the passages that you have read in the preceding pages.

1. *Homeric Hymns*, XXVII.
2. Triphiodorus, *The Capture of Troy*, 57-105.
3. Quintus Smyrnaeus, *The Fall of Troy*, XII, 521-551.
4. Lucian, *Icaromenippus*, 16-17.
5. Plutarch, *On Many Friends*, 3, selections
6. Seneca the Elder, *Controversiae*, 7-8.
7. Polybius, *History*, VI, 9.
8. Valerius Maximus, *Memorable Deeds and Sayings*, VIII, 13, ext. 1.
9. Callimachus, *Epigrams*, 2.
10. Catullus, *Poems*, 2, 3.
11. Ovid, *Amores*, II, 6.
12. Vergil, *Georgics*, II, 458-540.
13. Tibullus, I, 10.

14. Sappho in Dionysius of Halicanarssus *On Literary Composition*, XXIII.
15. Sulpicia in Tibullus, III, 13-17.
16. Hippocrates, *Aphorisms*, 1.
17. Pliny the Elder, *Natural History*, VII, 36.
18. Scribonius Largus, *Compositiones*, 59-60.
19. Simonides, in Herodotus, *Histories*, VII, 228.
20. Nepos, *The Excellent Commanders of Foreign Peoples*, XXIII, Hannibal.
21. Cicero, *Philippics*, II, 41.
22. Cornelius Severus in Seneca the Elder, *Suasoriae*, 6,26.
23. Pliny the Younger, *Letters*, VI, 16 and 20.
24. Suetonius, *The Twelve Caesars*, I, The Divine Julius, 81-82.
25. Lucretius, *On the Nature of Things*, I, selections after 62.
26. Manilius, *Astronomicon*, IV, selections after 883.
27. Diogenes Laertius, *Lives and Opinions of Eminent Philosophers*, VI, 2.
28. Marcus Aurelius, *Meditations*, II, 17.
29. Apuleius, *Metamorphosis*, III, 21.
30. Petronius, *Satyricon*, 61-62.
31. Pliny the Younger, *Letters*, VII, 27.
32. Sophocles, *Oedipus the King*, 1186-1208.
33. Ovid, *Metamorphoses*, III, 351-510.
34. Pausanias, *Description of Greece*, v, 7, 3
35. Ovid, *Metamorphoses*, V, 575-641.
36. Servius, *Commentary of Book III on the Aeneid*, 694.
37. Horace, *Odes*, III, 13.
38. Cicero, *On Behalf of the Poet Archias*, VII, 16.
39. Longinus, *On the Sublime*, 35.
40. Seneca the Younger, *Medea*, 364-379.

INDEX

COLOPHON

Tobias Goodman attended Brown & Nichols School, and presented the Latin oration at the Harvard graduation. He practiced surgery as a board certified urologist for thirty-five years in Rhode Island. He has written medical papers and has been awarded United States patents. He has a broad range of interests including medical invention, photography, classics, public health, and the history of technology.

The text was set in Garamond, a typeface designed by Claude Garamond (1500-1561). His foundry in Paris was one of the most influential in the world. Garamond is a reworking of Aldus Manutius' De Aetna. Garamond had quite a revival in the 20th century with many popular variations. Adobe being the most widely used tanks to the digital revolution is typesetting. The display faces are Caslon for the running heads, American Typewriter for chapter numbers, and Calligraphic 810 for the heads and subheads.

This book was typeset by Rhode Island Book Composition, Kingston, Rhode Island and printed by Gasch Printing of Odenton, Maryland on acid free paper. ∞